RICKSHAW REPORTER

RICKSHAW REPORTER

George L. Peet

This is a facsimile edition of the book first published in 1985.

To Dorothy,
Who prompted, encouraged and made this work of old age possible.

© 2009 Estate of George Peet

This book was first published in 1985.
This facsimile edition published by Marshall Cavendish Editions
An imprint of Marshall Cavendish International
1 New Industrial Road, Singapore 536196

All rights reserved

No part of this publication may be reproduced, stored in a retrieval system or transmitted, in any form or by any means, electronic, mechanical, photocopying, recording or otherwise, without the prior permission of the copyright owner. Request for permission should be addressed to the Publisher, Marshall Cavendish International (Asia) Private Limited, 1 New Industrial Road, Singapore 536196. Tel: (65) 6213 9300, Fax: (65) 6285 4871. E-mail: genref@sg.marshallcavendish.com. Website: www.marshallcavendish.com/genref

The publisher makes no representation or warranties with respect to the contents of this book, and specifically disclaims any implied warranties or merchantability or fitness for any particular purpose, and shall in no events be liable for any loss of profit or any other commercial damage, including but not limited to special, incidental, consequential, or other damages.

Other Marshall Cavendish Offices
Marshall Cavendish Ltd. 5th Floor 32–38 Saffron Hill, London EC1N 8FH • Marshall Cavendish Corporation. 99 White Plains Road, Tarrytown NY 10591-9001, USA • Marshall Cavendish International (Thailand) Co Ltd. 253 Asoke, 12th Flr, Sukhumvit 21 Road, Klongtoey Nua, Wattana, Bangkok 10110, Thailand • Marshall Cavendish (Malaysia) Sdn Bhd, Times Subang, Lot 46, Subang Hi-Tech Industrial Park, Batu Tiga, 40000 Shah Alam, Selangor Darul Ehsan, Malaysia

Marshall Cavendish is a trademark of Times Publishing Limited

National Library Board Singapore Cataloguing in Publication Data
Peet, George L.
Rickshaw reporter / George L. Peet. – Singapore : Marshall Cavendish Editions, c2009.
p. cm.
ISBN-13 : 978-981-261-637-1 (pbk.)

1. Peet, George L. 2. Journalists – Singapore – Biography. 3. Singapore – Social life and customs. 4. Singapore – History – 1867-1942. I. Title.

PN5449
070.92 — dc22   OCN302308661

Printed in Singapore by Times Printers Pte Ltd

Contents

Preface	v
1. Another Age, Another World	9
2. The Centenary City	13
3. Down The Gangway	18
4. A Colonial Mouthpiece	25
5. The Old Journalism	31
6. The Governor's Book	35
7. A Eurasian Goes "Home"	39
8. Living In The Past	43
9. Dinner By Candlelight	49
10. The Dutch Wife And The Jamban	56
11. The Rickshaw Procession	64
12. Conscience?	70
13. The Last Of The Horse Age	76
14. Ager's Punkah	79
15. Ghosts Of Cecil Street	85
16. Tek Wee And Baba Malay	91
17. The Leader On The Poster	96
18. A Fantastic Round	100
19. The Square	106
20. Kling Street	110
21. The Old Godowns	115
22. Echoes In The Streets	122
23. Life In Cavenagh Road	131
24. The Unknown Highway	138

25. The River Route	143
26. Inside The Colour Bar	146
27. Tuans And Mems	154
28. Down The Line	161
29. Upcountry	166
30. The Johore Planters	171
31. Rural Rides	175
32. People And Places	182
33. The New Boy	192
34. The Establishment	198
35. History In The Files	205
36. The Beginning Of The End	211
37. Endpiece	217
38. A Personal Postscript	222

Preface

MY MEMORIES OF SINGAPORE begin as long ago as April, 1923, when I arrived from England to join the *Straits Times* as a junior reporter — five years after the Great War and four years after the city had celebrated its centenary as a British settlement. Commonplace as that experience would have been at any time between the wars, it takes on an almost fantastic quality in retrospect now — so vast is the gulf between the old and the new Singapore.

Except for a wonderful interlude in the early 1930s as the first *Straits Times* staff man in the Federated Malay States, I lived in Singapore until the fall of the city to the Japanese army on February 15, 1942; then during the war (in the internment camp) when the *Syonan Shimbun* was published in our office in Cecil Street; and finally after the war as the first editor of the resuscitated *Straits Times* (and the last in its Anglo-Malayan tradition).

But, whatever qualifications I may have had in local knowledge and journalistic talent, I did not have either the stamina or the personality for what were to be the most stormy and divisive years not only in the history of local journalism but of Singapore itself.

The Old Guard of the British colonial community, back from internment and once again in the seats of power in commerce, shipping and banking, expected the *Straits Times* to be what it had been before the war, identifying with their interests and fighting a rearguard action against the new forces of Asian nationalism, democracy and trades unionism.

But I was convinced that unless the *Straits Times* transformed its prewar image, and was seen by the Eurasian and Asian communities among whom the bulk of its circulation lay as a liberal, progressive, sympathetic and sensitive organ of public opinion, albeit still British-edited and British-controlled (through an inner circle of management shares), it had no future in the journalism of the new era. After six years of the daily editorial exercise of walking the tightrope between the old Right and the new Left, I could take it no longer — and fell off. I resigned from the *Straits Times*, several years before I normally would have done, and settled in Perth, Western Australia, a beautiful city with a delightful climate and a relaxed way of life, where I found the new lease of life that has enabled me to be writing this in old age today.

But this premature retirement from the place where the best years of my journalistic life had been spent had an aftermath in a sense of psychological exile for a long time, and Singapore continued to be the most interesting place on Earth to me — as it still is. However, I have been exceptionally fortunate in the opportunities I have had to see Singapore in successive phases of the amazing growth and development that has taken place there under Prime Minister Lee Kuan Yew and to renew journalistic and personal ties there.

Since independence I have been back several times — but now as a British oldtimer with a tourist visa from the Republic of Singapore, just like my old Japanese enemies and all the other foreigners on the Orchard Road boulevard; but, unlike them, seeing Singapore in a long perspective that must be unique in that cosmopolitan throng. There has been precious little nostalgia for the old days in these visits, but they have added up to a marvellous experience of contrasts and echoes for an old journalist of the British period; and each time I have gone back to

PREFACE vii

Perth with a fresh balance sheet of debits and credits for the old and the new Singapore.

With memories such as these, it is perhaps not surprising that family and friends press me to write what they are pleased to call "my memoirs" before it is too late — and they certainly are memories that must be very rare in the world today, and will soon vanish altogether.

Since I was not yet twenty-one when I first landed at Singapore from England in 1923, I am probably the last of the European community of which I then became a very junior member; and my contemporaries between the wars are almost all gone too. The Association of British Malaya, which used to hold that scattered community of people with a common Straits or F.M.S. background together from its headquarters in London, was wound up ten years ago (after having diplomatically changed its name to the British Association of Malaysia). Its monthly magazine, recalling familiar names and nostalgic place-names, has gone too. The *Straits Times Annual* is posted as a Christmas gift to fewer and fewer people overseas every year.

So this effort of mine in old age is the swan-song of an almost extinct breed of colonial man. However, I am no longer interested in writing the sort of personal and political memoirs that a bygone European community would have expected from a *Straits Times* journalist of their time.

What does interest me now is the vanished Singapore that I see in the mirror of my own mind and if I can recapture some of those reflections for the Singaporeans of today, what better legacy could an old colonial journalist hope to leave behind than that! When I lived in Singapore between the wars I used to enjoy reading the old and out-of-print books left behind by my British predecessors, reflecting different periods of local history and social change from the 1840s onwards.

In my day there had been no break in the continuity of local history such as that marked by the Japanese occupation of three and a half years during the World War, and the consequent end of the colonial period. In the 1920s and 1930s it was still essentially the same Singapore that it had been during the 19th Century. But when I go back now I am hard put to it to find anything left of the Singapore of my time except the names of the streets and such bits of the British period as the National Trust is preserving for posterity.

The lesser folk of the Asian communities who in my time used to live in pleasant little bungalows along the lorongs, the narrow laterite lanes winding through suburbs of high bamboo hedges and coconut palms and fruit trees, leading off Geylang Road or Serangoon Road, or in quiet streets of terrace houses within a five-minute stroll of the beach at Katong or Siglap, are now a new population of flat-dwellers.

Is it possible that if I succeed in adding my contribution, I can communicate something like the pleasure I found in those old books to readers living in the completely new and different Singapore of today? I am encouraged to think so because I see there not only a new life-style but a concern with the quality of life, as well as the economy that is the basis of it all.

I see too in Singapore a new publishing industry, a wider reading public, and a revived interest in the past reflected in the new local literature. The anti-colonial reaction of the first heady years after independence has ebbed and the Singapore of the Raffles tradition is beginning to be seen with the same intellectual detachment as the Singhapura of Sri Vijaya and Majapahit.

If I use personal reminiscence only in so far as it reflects the period — leaving the heavy stuff to the academic historians (who were not there), and the topical gossip to the ghosts of my contemporaries — perhaps readers will find this garrulous old-timer an entertaining companion after all.

1
Another Age, Another World

ONE DAY IN 1923, when I was nearly twenty-one and a junior reporter on the *Essex County Standard*, I saw an advertisement in a London newspaper that remains imprinted upon my brain to this day:

> *Junior Reporter for English-language daily in the Straits Settlements. Three-year agreement. Salary $300 - 350 - 400 p.m. Six months Home leave on full pay. Second-class passage paid. Outfit allowance.*

The Straits Settlements ...... I knew nothing whatever about them except that they were a British colony in a region that was a complete blank in my mental map of the Far East. But I did not try to find out more precisely where and what the Straits Settlements were before answering that advertisement. This was a job in the East, and that was enough.

I was asked to go up to London for an interview, and was then told that the anonymous newspaper was the *Straits Times*, of Singapore, and that the job was mine. The middle-aged Englishman who interviewed me was himself a member of the *Straits Times* staff, H.L. Hopkin — Hoppy, as he was known to his many friends on the *Bangkok Daily Mail* in his early days, and later in Singapore — who was staying in London during Home leave with his family.

Going back to Colchester in the train that afternoon I realised that I had only a vague idea where Singapore was. I knew it was an important port somewhere on the farther side of the Indian Ocean, and the proposed site for a new British naval base in the Far East. But that was all I did know about the place.

As an apprentice journalist I was an avid reader of the London papers, and I still remember a *Daily Telegraph* heading: BATTLE-SHIPS FOR SINGAPORE. That must have been about 1922, but it was as yet only a proposal. I was evidently not interested enough to study the sketch-map that must have illustrated the report.

However, when I said goodbye to the *Essex County Standard* and went back to London, I did what little I could to correct my ignorance. The small Malay States Information Agency in Cannon Street, in the City, had nothing to offer to a young man going out there for the first time. But on advice received there I bought the only book about the Straits Settlements and the Malay States that was available at Hatchard's, the Oxford Street bookshop which specialised in Far Eastern literature. This was *British Malaya* by Sir Frank Swettenham, and my copy bore the date 1922, but that was misleading, for this was the fourth edition of a book which was first published in 1905 and had never been revised since. Even so, it was the standard work on the country, and the only one of any sort about Malaya still in print after the Great War. However, there was no time during those last few days of family farewells in Cornwall to do more than glance between the covers at this new world now opening up ahead of me.

Singapore was nearly a month away when I sailed from Liverpool, a remote and little-known place in the Far East for the vast majority of British people at a time when middle-class families did not even cross the Channel for their summer seaside holidays, when a vast gulf still existed between East and West not only in time and space but in the minds of men.

I was booked to sail by the S.S *Glaucus,* of the Blue Funnel

Line; and, for some reason that I cannot now recall, I was expecting a glamorous Eastern liner. But when I found the *Glaucus* in dock at Birkenhead, and went up the gangway, I saw at once that she was unmistakably a cargo ship; and, what made the disillusionment worse, she had just finished coaling, so the iron deck on to which I stepped was still black and gritty with coaldust. It was before oil replaced coal in the merchant fleets of the world. On a liner the dirty work would have been done before the passengers came on board. The next morning, however, life looked brighter. I went out on deck to find that we were steaming off the coast of Wales over a calm sea; and the *Glaucus* was herself again, trim and shipshape for the long run to Japanese ports, as befitted the famous line to which she belonged.

For me those memories remain as sharp and clear as colour photographs to this day — a perfect view of Lands End a few miles off on a sunny morning, and that last farewell to the green fields of Cornwall ..... the Straits of Gibraltar ..... the unbelievable blue of the Mediterranean under spring skies ..... the flat skyline of Port Said coming up like the horizon of a new world.

The *Glaucus* coaled again at Port Said for the run across the Indian Ocean; and in these days of mechanised ports it is hard to believe that we watched a long line of Arabs, their faces and arms black with coaldust, coming along a pontoon bridge from the wharf, carrying the coal in containers on their backs, in and out of the hold in an endless chain like human ants.

The 24-hour passage through the Suez Canal, riding high above vast and empty deserts on either side, was an unforgettable experience (even more mysterious under the stars than by day). The run down the Red Sea is another good memory, with the friendly deck officers of the *Glaucus* pointing out Mount Sinai and other landmarks on the Arabian and African coasts.

But the Indian Ocean was another story. The *Glaucus* did not call at Colombo, as the liners always did, so there was no break in the monotony of that ten-day crossing to Penang. In the humid heat under the deck awnings, rolling in the ocean swells, the four passengers — all young fellows like myself, going out to their first job in the East — had to kill time as best they could while the officers and crew of the *Glaucus* went about their duties.

After leaving Suez I got out *British Malaya* from my cabin trunk, and during that long, boring run across the Indian Ocean, free from the distractions of liner saloons that might well have interfered with my homework, I tried to spend an hour or two with Sir Frank Swettenham every day. He was heavy reading for anyone who did not already have a Malayan background, but by the time we passed Achin Head I had taken the first step in my Anglo-Malayan education, though I still had almost everything to learn.

On the way down the Straits of Malacca the *Glaucus* called at Penang and Port Swettenham. And after another day and night it was early morning when the *Glaucus* rounded the west coast of Singapore Island and arrived at Tanjong Pagar.

In almost complete silence two tugs nudged the ship into her berth at an almost empty wharf. There was time to note the lovely colour in the deep-green sunlit water, the low ridge dotted with Harbour Board bungalows and spacious compounds seen above the godown roofs, the unforgettable scent of the Eastern tropics diffusing over the water off an island that was still a rural countryside or jungle all the way from the Straits of Johore, and richly green in the city suburbs too.

That is a rare picture of ugly utilitarian Tanjong Pagar in my mental album of Singapore that I would have missed had I arrived, as nearly all my contemporaries did, amid the bustle and confusion of a liner berthing at a wharf crowded with people waiting to meet the ship. But those are the reflections of old age, not of the nervous and self-conscious young newcomer who was myself on the deck of the *Glaucus* that morning.

The Centenary City

I HAD JUST ARRIVED IN TIME to see Singapore as it was when it was just over a hundred years old as a port-city of the modern world, but before all the social, technological and strategic changes that transformed it during the period between the Great War and the World War.

Both in its outward appearance and in its inner life it was the Singapore that had celebrated Centenary Day — February 6, 1919 — when the leaders of all the racial communities had joined with colonial officials and British merchants in honouring the founder, Sir Stamford Raffles, and in gratitude for a hundred years of peace and prosperity in which his settlement had grown from a Malay fishing kampong at the mouth of the Singapore River, and a few clearings of Chinese gambier planters on the forested hills behind it, to a city of nearly half a million people and the twelfth port in the world.

Even its historical link with the ancient world across five centuries of oblivion had re-entered the consciousness of modern Singapore through the celebrations on Centenary Day — for was it not the haunting Sanskrit place-name of Singhapura at the tip of the Malay Peninsula, tolling like a bell down the centuries from the Indianised empires of Java and Sumatra, and heard again in the old Malay chronicles that Sir Stamford Raffles had studied in Malacca and Penang, that led him to the obscure kampong of that name on the other side of the Singapore Strait from the Rhio Archipelago?

The local history, the traditions, the personal stories of the East India Company regime and the later Crown colony has been carefully collected and preserved in that literary labour of love, the two volumes of *One Hundred Years of Singapore,* and in the companion volume, *One Hundred Years of the Chinese in Singapore,* by that fine Straits Chinese scholar and community leader, Sir Song Ong Siang.

But none of the cosmopolitan population that watched the solemn ceremonies and joined the festivities of Centenary Day called themselves Singaporeans. They thought and spoke of themselves only in terms of their own racial compartments: the Chinese (divided into the China-born and the Straits-born), the Indians (the same dividing line between immigration and domicile there), the Malays (again that dividing line, for most of those wearing their national costume and the Muslim cap had come from Indonesia), the Eurasians, who were more British than the British if they were of that descent, but not quite so much so if the white ancestor had lived in Portuguese or Dutch Malacca.

The English-educated Asiatic* public represented in all those communities (except the Malays) — that is to say, the Straits-born Chinese, the local-born Indians and Ceylonese, and a few Jewish, Armenian and Persian families as well — might sometimes speak of themselves as citizens of Singapore when they took part in civic assemblages such as Centenary Day; but never as "Singaporeans". Any such personal identification with the place would have sounded odd and forced at that time, for

---

* From now on I shall be using the terminology of my time — words like "Asiatic" which may raise readers' eyebrows or even anti-colonial hackles without this apologia, since they are no longer heard or not permissible in the democratic Singapore of today. In retrospect, this local lingo seems one of the more curious aspects of life in a vanished Singapore, and we shall be looking at it again later.

although the local-born might feel strongly attached to Singapore, as many did, it was not their city in any political or national sense but a British colonial possession, the capital of the Straits Settlements.

The older European residents in 1919 had all lived in Singapore before and during the 1914 - 18 war, and in the formal addresses and speeches of Centenary Day one could sense a realisation in their community that things would never be the same again, that great but as yet unknown changes would come in the new era that was opening up for Singapore and for East and West. But happily for all the Europeans, Eurasians and Asiatics who joined in the celebrations on that day there were no premonitions of what the second century of local history had in store for Singapore. Indeed, confidence in its future as a British possession and in the power of the British Empire to protect it had never been more unquestioning than at that historic anniversary after the Great War.

During the four years of war in Europe and the Middle East the Japanese navy had taken over from the Royal Navy in protecting British interests in and around the Pacific and the Indian Ocean, thanks to the Anglo-Japanese Alliance. "We could have taken this place ..." remarked a Japanese admiral visiting the port during the war years (or so a colleague once told me). Instead of that, the Japanese cruiser *Otawa* actually rushed to the relief of Singapore after the mutiny of an Indian sepoy regiment in 1915. In 1919 the Anglo-Japanese Treaty was still in force, so on Centenary Day there was not the slightest cloud on the horizon in the direction of Japan.

At those celebrations, in the afterglow of the Allied victory in Europe in 1918, there had been high hopes among the British and Chinese and Indian merchants that with the lifting of wartime controls on shipping and commerce there would now be a speedy return to prosperity in the import and export trade. But in 1920 the bottom suddenly dropped out of the rubber market, the yard-stick of the Singapore economy as it was then; and all plans to catch up with civic and business arrears, and for new development, had to be put back on the shelf, where they had been during the four years of war.

Tanjong Pagar, where I had landed, was actually the only part of Singapore where there had been any major development since before the Great War. Because its shipments of tin and rubber were vital to the war effort of the British Empire, the completion of what was known as the Tanjong Pagar docks scheme was the one exception permitted to the freeze on large public works during the war years.

This scheme, which had been started in 1908, was completed in 1917 with the formal opening of the Empire Dock, constructed in what had been a tidal lagoon behind the old wooden wharves that had served the port since steamers began to take over from sailing ships. The Empire Dock is itself an echo of the old colonial regime, for it was so named by the Governor, Sir Arthur Young, because the last payment to the contractors had been made on Empire Day — May 24 — a date in the local calendar that was then observed in the Straits Settlements, particularly in the schools.

The rubber slump was already lifting and business optimism reviving when I arrived in early 1923, but it was still the Singapore of the Centenary, for there had been practically no change in the city and suburbs since then, except that there were now more cars among the rickshaws and the bullock carts.

In fact, the city had remained virtually unaltered since war broke out in Europe in 1914; and the life-style of the various racial communities in the suburbs had not changed either — again, except for the senior Europeans and some of the more affluent Asiatic families who now had a car instead of a carriage in the stables of their compound houses; but even they could only use their cars in the city.

In this perspective we can see farther back than that, for my first year or two in Singapore were the last in which the place retained its essential character as the purely commercial port and colonial Settlement of the 19th Century, with a garrison only for local defence; the last of Singapore before the Naval Base, before the air age, before the full onset of the motor age, before the Causeway, before the new journalism ended the old isolation from the outside world and from the Malayan hinterland.

But remember that this is a view of colonial Singapore in which the viewer is wearing white blinkers. Anyone growing up in a Eurasian or Straits Chinese or other local-born family in my younger years would have quite different memories, which I know nothing about though I hope they are being recorded in the National University of Singapore and in new local literature. Even so, the year 1923 seems a peculiarly astrological one on which to begin reflections on the history I have seen in the making of Singapore ever since, for on September 16, 1923, at No. 92 Kampong Java Road, there was born to a young employee of the Shell Company and his 16-year old wife a son whom they named Lee Kuan Yew.

3
Down The Gangway

MY FIRST DAY IN SINGAPORE IN 1923 ... an unforgettable day for me, as it evidently was for my dead-and-gone contemporaries, since they always began their reminiscences with it. And here I am, following in their footsteps in 1983. But could it be of interest to anybody living in Singapore today? I think it may be, for it presents the first of innumerable contrasts between past and present, a prosaic little period sketch in itself, an introduction to the new way of life for the reader as it was for me.

When the *Glaucus* went alongside, a European in white suit and topee who had been waiting on the wharf sought me out on deck and introduced himself as Ager, of the *Straits Times*. He was an Englishman many years my senior, and was in fact the general manager of the Straits Times Press Ltd. That is a first indication of what a small organisation it then was. Ager's successors at the managerial desk between the wars would never have dreamt of going to Tanjong Pagar to meet a ship bringing a new recruit to the editorial staff. But there was no-one in the office to whom the manager could have delegated that duty, so small was the *Straits Times* staff when I joined it.

However, there was probably a kindly personal motive as well as an official one for Ager's shepherding me around on that Saturday morning, for he himself had memories of arriving from Home as a young reporter, having gone over to management later in his career.

My first impression as we crossed the wharf to Ager's car was that the humid heat of Singapore was even fiercer than I had expected — and that is not as banal a reminiscence as it might seem, for it is a reminder that the rayon-type fabrics now used for tropical clothing did not then exist (and in fact did not come into the shops until after the World War).

I was dressed for this important occasion in what had been my Sunday-best at Colchester: a heavy English woollen suit, complete with waistcoat, a watch-chain draped across it to a large watch in the fob pocket. (The wrist-watch for men was just taking on in England, and would have been regarded as a rather foppish new fashion in Colchester.)

However, if I had been a more sophisticated or more affluent traveller I could have had a more suitable suit for a hot climate made by a London tailor — linen or flannel, or what was known for some reason as "white sharkskin" (associated in those days with Hollywood film stars.)

The *Straits Times* manager's car was not all like the shiny status symbols that are required of company executives in Singapore today, but was an open tourer with canvas hood that had plainly seen some years' service. The syce — an Anglo-Indian word of the horse age that was still used for a car driver — was a Malay, wearing *sarong* and *baju*, with the black velvet cap, the *songkok*, that was the emblem of his Muslim faith. "*Balek, Straits Times*"*, said Ager to his syce in bazaar Malay. Very few men and woman in the Malay community of Singapore had been to an English-language school in those days.

At the old *Straits Times* building in Cecil Street, I was introduced to an English sub-editor, E.A. Snewin, and my new editor, A.W. Still. The only other member of the editorial staff, a Eurasian reporter, was out at the time. The *Straits Times,* a sizeable and important paper, had been produced by one sub-editor and one reporter, with a bit of amateur sports coverage, during the six months that Hoppy (still in London) was away on leave.

---

*"Back to the Straits Times"

On that first morning Snewin gave me a quick tour of the building while Ager caught up with his own work, and that memory is journalistic history now. First we went downstairs to the ground floor, where Snewin proudly showed me the new electrically operated flatbed printing press, a technical advance on anything in Malayan newspaper offices at the time. "Prints ten thousand copies an hour" he said. But that was far more than the *Straits Times* actually printed at the time. (Singapore had as yet no Sunday paper, and the only other *Straits Times* publication was the weekly *Straits Budget,* made up of selections from the daily for former readers living in retirement overseas).

Snewin pointed to a small machine, rather like the mangle used by British housewives on washing day, in a corner of the machine-room. "That was what they used to print the paper on in the old days," he said. "By turning a handle, one copy at a time." Years later I learnt that Ager actually saw that little handpress in use when he joined the *Straits Times* in 1898. It was worked by two Tamil coolies, who were paid eight dollars a month — "and glad to get it," he said. That was in the old *Straits Times* office (the second in its history), at the corner of Finlayson Green and Robinson Road. But soon after Ager arrived the handpress was superseded by what he described as "an oilburner" (electricity not yet being available in the city.) It was already a museum piece in Cecil Street, of course; and it should have been preserved for Raffles Museum (as the State Museum of today was then called), but it vanished during further modernisation between the wars.

But more of journalism in Cecil Street later.

Ager now drove me up to town, and first to the old G.P.O. to post my shipboard letters — a reminder to readers in the air age that they would not reach my parents in Cornwall until a month later, after that long slow crawl across half of the globe by sea. Ager's syce had no difficulty in parking in the small open space of Fullerton Square, and we left him there while Ager took me into the Hongkong and Shanghai Bank (another building that vanished long ago) to open a bank account.

That was a surprise, as a cheque-book was the last thing I had ever thought of a few weeks before. A newly arrived European assistant had to be introduced at the bank by a senior man in his firm, but a word from the *Straits Times* manager was enough. Already a sense of an entirely new social and racial status was beginning to inflate the ego, and transform the young Englishman into a junior member of the British colonial community.

Ager next took me to a Chinese tailor in High Street. He addressed the tailor as Wing Loong, and it was obvious that they knew each other very well in a business way. Ager had been with the *Straits Times* for quarter of a century, and Wing Loong had been born in Singapore and educated at one of the English-language schools of the Colonial Government or the missions. He was one or more generations away from his family origins in South China.

After taking my measurements Wing Loong asked how many suits he should make, and I was staggered to hear Ager advise me to order twelve. "You really need more than that," he said, "but better not run up any more debts than you have to at first." The suits were of white cotton drill, and a fresh suit had to be put on every day. They were sent to the laundry once a week, so one had to have the next week's supply in hand while the soiled suits were with the dhoby. My initial order only provided for a six-day week, with no change at weekends. However, it would have to do for the time being.

But now I was in for yet another surprise. How was I to pay for all those suits? No problem! "*Straits Times,* Wing Loong", said Ager genially and the firm's name seemed to be a magical talisman of credit for the newcomer. The beaming, bespectacled Wing Loong nodded as if to say "Of course .....", wrote out his account there and then, and presented it for me to sign. And so I signed my first chit. There was no question of a down payment. The price of the suits was $14 each — the Straits dollar being then about eight to the pound sterling — and I would pay off the account at $50 a month.

Wing Loong was not his real name, only his business name,

but I am sure that Ager did not know that. True citizens of Singapore though they both were in their separate ways, they had never met socially, and they never would. Weddings would be the only occasions, apart from formal public gatherings, when Europeans and Asians would ever meet socially. For Ager and Wing Loong there were no social bridges that they could have crossed in homes or clubs, even if they had wanted to — which they almost certainly would not have done. A decade later, however, I knew Wing Loong by his real name of Ng Sen Choy, and we were meeting on a basis of racial and social equality. But more of that when I come to the second decade between the wars.

From High Street we went back to Raffles Place and into the department store of Robinson and Co. for me to buy a topee. Evidently this was one of the first essentials, for every European on the sidewalks in Battery Road and Raffles Place was wearing one. Ager advised me never to go out without my topee during the day between nine and five. Belief in the reality of sunstroke as an ever-present danger for white people in the Malayan climate was then universal and unquestioned; and that fallacy was not finally destroyed until we learnt to live like Malay peasants and Chinese coolies in the Japanese internment camp.

My topee was a truly imposing piece of headgear. It was white, with a curved extension at the back to protect the nape of the neck (thought to be particularly vulnerable), and shaped like the khaki sun-helmets you see British soldiers wearing on the march in India in television films of Rudyard Kipling's stories. My topee had a white band around the base, a leather sweat-lining inside where it fitted around the head, a chin strap, a sort of button on top, and around the button three holes, presumably for ventilation. (I once saw something like an earwig emerge from one of those holes, so there must have been a hollow interior.)

The English shop assistant offered an alternative type, which some men preferred. This had a longer and narrower shape, projecting in front and at the back. It was made of cork or some other light wood, covered with pale-green cloth, and was much lighter than the military type. It was also much cheaper. But the white helmet type appealed to me at once as more symbolic of my new colonial and Eastern image, and I had no hesitation in rejecting the less romantic one. My topee bore a brand name well known to British people in India and elsewhere in the East — Heath's, of Bond Street, London; and the price was a stiff $17.

Finally Ager drove me to the boarding house in Cavenagh Road where I was to stay, and after introducing me to the proprietor and manageress, Mrs Matthews, he left me there and went back to the office. Mrs Matthews told me that she was giving me a room at $150 a month, which included all meals but not my room-boy, whom I would have to pay myself. However, she said, I could economise by sharing a "boy" with the chap in the next room. Another extra would be the dhoby. So there was more than half my monthly salary gone already. But I did not know then how difficult it would be to make ends meet on the other half.

My memories of Ager's kindness on my first day do not end there, for he called for me on his way home and took me back with him for tiffin — it being only a half-day at the office — and that afternoon Mrs Ager gave me much kind and motherly advice on how to live in Singapore, and particularly on $300 a month. The only point that remains in my memory now is that marriage would be out of the question until my fifth or sixth year — if I stayed that long.

That was Saturday, and Wing Loong had promised to deliver the first two white suits as soon as they were ready, to let me get out of my hot English suit as quickly as possible. Sure enough, a rickshaw arrived at the boarding house with a parcel on Monday: two white suits cut and sewn during the weekend, starched, pressed and ready to wear. The puller had trotted a mile with the parcel, including the steep rise up Cavenagh Road, and there was no delivery charge. The remainder of my order followed during the week in similar instalments. There's service for you — and sweated labour too!

Even now I was not yet completely fitted out for this colonial way of life, as I soon discovered.

During my first week on the *Straits Times* a small British touring company was due to open at the Victoria Theatre on Saturday night with a season of plays from the West End of London, and Snewin instructed me to attend in a new role as theatre critic. This was absurd, for my only experience of the theatre had been at the Hippodrome in Colchester High Street, which confined itself to touring revues and variety entertainment. I do not think I had ever seen a serious play. But what Snewin failed to tell me was that I could not go to the theatre in my English lounge suit. When it became known in my boarding house on that Saturday afternoon that I had to attend the play at the Victoria Theatre, and that I did not possess a dinner jacket, there was a general flurry. (In England I had never owned a dinner suit, or moved in the classes of society that dressed for dinner). One or two of my fellow-boarders rushed around, borrowing a black dinner jacket here, a pair of black trousers there, shiny dress shoes, a dress shirt (with cuff links), stiff collar (with back and front studs) and black tie. These contributions were hastily fitted on, or replaced with others if need be; and that evening after dinner the boarding house sent me off to the theatre in a rickshaw, properly dressed for the occasion.

The *Straits Times* office was two miles away on the other side of town, and there was no bus service, but Mrs Matthews — who was local-born, and knew how to live in Singapore, and exactly what should be paid for everything — quickly solved my transport problem by hiring a rickshaw puller on a monthly contract ($12 a month, if memory serves.) For that he took me to the office in the morning, and was waiting outside the office to bring me back at five o'clock in the afternoon. In between, he was free to earn whatever extra fares he could find.

Hoppy arrived back from leave a week or so later, and put me up for the Cricket Club and the Swimming Club. That was routine for every new European assistant; but again it was an aspect of life for which there had been no equivalent in my life in lodgings in Colchester. I felt very much the new boy in the colonial school.

4
A Colonial Mouthpiece

THE *STRAITS TIMES* was then an afternoon paper, and remained so throughout the period between the wars. In 1923 it was pre-eminently the leading newspaper in Singapore, and the only one that could claim a scattered but influential readership in Malaya as a whole.

The circulation figures were never published — not even revealed inside the office, for when I inquired shortly after joining the paper the evasive answer I got was "about 5,500". Judging by the short run that one would hear rumbling in the machine-room below our floor when the paper went to press at one o'clock, that figure would be about right.

But the principal advertisers — the import and export firms, the department stores, the motor firms, the cinemas — did not need to know the precise circulation figures, since they already knew that these were at saturation point for the European community in which they themselves lived, and whose purchasing power at various levels they knew very well too.

Miniscule as that circulation must seem to the *Straits Times* staff of today, it would be a most misleading anachronism to read anything more into it than that comparison, for the *Straits Times* of 1923 was not only regarded in the Singapore share market as practically a gilt-edged investment, but was at the high point of its influence as a journal of opinion in colonial times.

The *Straits Times* was not yet sold on the streets then, but was taken around the offices by Indian and Malay sellers about two o'clock, after the tiffin hour. There were several newsagents' shops in Battery Road and Raffles Place at which the paper could be bought, and it was also on sale at the European hotels: the Europe, the Raffles and the Adelphi. A small van engaged on contract took parcels of papers around the town.

There were a few hundred European subscribers upcountry, all the way from Johore to Penang and Kedah, and they would get their paper a day or two late, particularly on the rubber estates. Those readers would be at the top level of the Malayan Civil Service and management in British commercial, planting and mining companies. But as the *Straits Times* news service was no better than that of the *Malay Mail* in Kuala Lumpur, the *Times of Malaya* in Ipoh and the two Penang dailies, the *Straits Echo* and the *Pinang Gazette,* the only reason why these upcountry subscribers took the *Straits Times* was that its editor had a country-wide reputation as a leader writer on political and economic affairs, especially the rubber plantation industry.

The *Straits Times* was regarded not only by its readers but by the Singapore public in general as definitely a European paper; and I am sure that the editor and his staff — even more positively the directors and shareholders — never thought of it as anything else.

On the fringe of the *Straits Times* circulation in Singapore was a sprinkling of non-European readers: Eurasian and Straits-born Chinese professional men — lawyers, doctors, bankers, accountants — a few Indian businessmen, perhaps a dozen leading Jewish, Persian and Arab residents as well. So few were these Westernised figures in the professional and public life of Singapore at that time that one knew the names of most of them from memory.

On my first day in the office the editor, an old hand in Eastern journalism, called me into his sanctum for a kindly welcome and an introductory talk on reporting in Singapore, as compared with Colchester. He told me that I would be working among a British commercial community in and around Raffles Place — merchants and their staffs, accountants, lawyers, doctors and so on; and he thought I would have no trouble in fitting in there, socially or otherwise. "Of course," he added, "there are the Harbour Board people as well, but they stay in their own area, and we never see anything of them." I do not recall that the editor mentioned the Government officers in Empress Place, on the other side of the Singapore River; but I am quite sure that he did not refer to Asiatic readers at all.

"The one indispensable requisite for editing a newspaper in Singapore," said the famous A.W. Still to his new recruit, "is a keen commercial intelligence." Well, he certainly had that; but it was just as well that there was no crystal ball on his desk, for whatever other qualifications I may have had when I occupied that editorial chair later in my career, rapport with British Big Business was unhappily not one of them.

Straits Times profits and dividends were never published, but they must have been highly satisfactory, for if a line of *Straits Times* shares came on the market — which rarely happened — they were quickly snapped up. It had been a limited company since 1900, but it did not publish an annual report; and if an annual meeting of shareholders was held, the only people who knew about it were themselves. However, everybody at the managerial level of the British commercial community knew who the *Straits Times* directors were (and probably hobnobbed with them at the Singapore Club every day).

Shares could be transferred only with the consent of the board of directors, the object of that provision being to ensure that control of the *Straits Times* remained in the right hands — from the directors' point of view, and that of British mercantile interests in the port. This was also a safeguard to ensure that the *Straits Times* remained identified with the colonial regime as a whole, that it would be the mouthpiece of official and unofficial British interests in local politics, as opposed to the domiciled communities — the Eurasians, the Straits-born Chinese and others — if and when any such issue called for comment.

That was the basic position, never articulated but taken for granted, that any editor of the *Straits Times* had to maintain. But that did not mean that under a great editor of Still's calibre, enlightened and broadminded for his time in Eastern colonial society, there could not be a choice between a liberal or a conservative viewpoint, between progress or reaction in editorial policy.

Anyone curious enough to go back, as I have done, to the article headed "Singapore's Future" which Still wrote in 1919 as an epilogue to the two Centenary volumes, *One Hundred Years of Singapore,* in which he reflects on Chinatown slums and educational policy and other challenges of the present and the future, will see in that article the social conscience in a British colonial voice and mind.

The largest *Straits Times* shareholder was said to be the French Roman Catholic Mission (no doubt an investment dating back to the last century); and another large parcel of shares was held by two old ladies in England who had never been out East, but had inherited their holding from one of the early proprietors of the *Straits Times*. Several of the old-established British mercantile firms of the Colony and the great Eastern banks represented in Singapore were also believed to be shareholders; and it is a safe guess that they were the shareholders who really counted with the board of directors.

The *Straits Times* was nearly as old as Singapore itself, having been founded in 1845 by R.C. Woods, a lawyer from Calcutta, when the Settlement had existed for only twenty-six years as a trading station of the East India Company. Since then, the *Straits Times* had played a prominent and often contentious role in local history under several exceptionally able editors, of whom A.W. Still, my first editor, was the most distinguished of all.

The morning paper, the *Singapore Free Press,* whose office was in Robinson Road, was also British-owned and a European paper in the same sense as the *Straits Times*. It was an even older paper, having been founded in 1834; and in 1923 it was still managing to keep going comfortably on a modest advertising revenue and with a much smaller circulation than the *Straits Times*. Even so, the *Free Press* was quite influential in a more parochial way, for its editor, Walter Makepeace, had been with the paper since 1877 — and in Malacca before that. Makepeace was not comparable with Still as a leader writer, but he commented upon current affairs in the perspective of half a century.

There was another English-language daily, the *Malaya Tribune*, which was published down an alley off Battery Road. It was also an afternoon newspaper, and so was nominally our rival, but when it was mentioned in European circles it was likely to be referred to rather contemptuously as "the kranis' paper" (the clerks' paper); and it literally was that, because it sold at five cents, against ten cents for the *Straits Times* — and five cents a day saved on a newspaper meant a lot on clerical pay in those days.

The *Tribune*, had been founded in 1915, after several unsuccessful Eurasian efforts to get a truly local newspaper going which would counterbalance the European Press. The moving spirit behind that enterprise was Dr Lim Boon Keng, the outstanding leader of the Straits-born Chinese in Singapore; and he was able to enlist Chinese capital, also some Eurasian backing. It was intended to be a mouthpiece for the domiciled English-speaking communities, the people born and bred in Singapore, who regarded the place as their home, as the Europeans spoke of Home.

Most certainly there was a need for such a mouthpiece in local affairs. But so far the *Malaya Tribune* had not gained much ground. It was hardly paying its way, since its low-paid readership did not attract the big European advertisers; and politically it was ineffective, because the local-born communities had yet to produce a journalist sufficiently competent and forceful to win the respect of the colonial Establishment.

Consequently the proprietors had to employ European journalists to edit the paper, and, however sincerely these leader writers might voice local grievances and champion local causes, they were not identified in the public eye with the people whom the *Tribune* represented. These British editors were, outside the

Tribune office, members of the colonial community themselves.

Technically, the *Tribune* was a poor production, and it was not regarded as a serious competitor to the *Straits Times* — in fact, not as a competitor at all. Yet it was potentially the most significant enterprise in Singapore journalism at that time, though it would have been too much to expect the prewar European oldtimers who headed the British firms and the British administration to see that. Even at that early stage the *Tribune* represented a nascent force of local opinion that was to present a serious and gathering challenge to British authoritarian rule (and incidentally, to the *Straits Times* as well) in the decade before the World War.

In looking at Singapore journalism as it was at that time one has to bear in mind that (outside the European community) the local English-speaking public, or rather, the English-educated — for it was not necessarily the same thing in family life at that stage of the Colony's social history — was still a very limited one. Apart from a few middleclass professional and business people, it consisted of what was then referred to as "the clerical class" — chiefly Eurasians and Straits-born Chinese employed in the European firms as clerks and shop assistants, or in the Government departments and Municipal offices. There were also some English-educated Indians and Ceylonese of the same social class, local-born as well as immigrant.

Outside this narrow field of employment it was not necessary to know English, since the Chinese dealers who bought imported goods from the European firms or sold tropical produce to them carried on their transactions in bazaar Malay. The field open to newspaper enterprise and competition was thus equally narrow. As for the vernacular Press — several very large and influential Chinese daily newspapers (all set up by hand, with five thousand characters on the shelf in front of the compositor), and one or two small and struggling Indian and Malay dailies — they were outside our world altogether.

The Old Journalism

THE *STRAITS TIMES* was quite an impressive-looking newspaper by any standards in 1923: twelve pages of the old broadsheet size — which was twenty-two inches deep — going up to sixteen pages once or twice a week, and packed with advertisements.

It was cleanly printed, produced by experienced journalists (within the narrow limits of an oldfashioned style and layout that had not changed since before the Great War); and the proofreading would have put the quality newspapers of present-day Fleet Street to shame.

However, if you looked more closely you would see that there was surprisingly little overseas news in the *Straits Times* and only scanty local or upcountry news, no feature material whatever, and a good deal of scissors-and-paste padding in the back pages. Even so, that represented quite a lot of work for the tiny sub-editorial staff then employed.

The *Straits Times* in fact reflected the life of a European community in which everybody in Raffles Place knew everybody else by sight, if not by name, and in which there was often nothing outside the courts and sport for the most investigative of reporters to write about.

The *Straits Times* reflected something else: a European community that knew very little of what was happening in the outside world. The Reuters news service from London consisted of perhaps a dozen brief items a day, leaded out by the printer, with lots of white space between headings, to make it look more than it really was. It was cabled in a special condensed jargon which had to be expanded by the sub-editor so as to make ten lines of journalistic "cablese" look like twenty lines of readable English. The cable news, padded out like this, filled about three columns of the main news page.

Cable rates were so high that even a prosperous Eastern newspaper like the *Straits Times* could only afford the minimum Reuter Service. The Empire Press rate of "a-penny-a-word" did not come in until some years later, and that brought an immediate and great improvement in the flow of news from Britain to the Colonies and the Dominions.

The *Straits Times* had a correspondent in London — in the Press Gallery of the House of Commons, where he reported (as a sideline to his regular job) any debates of special interest to Malaya and sent them on by sea mail, where they would be read in Singapore as old news. He also wrote a weekly London Letter. But only for Malayan news of the highest importance could he go to the expense of sending a cable.

For its regional and upcountry news the *Straits Times* relied upon such contributions as "Notes From Siam", "Jottings From Java", "Penang Notes", "Malacca Notes" and so on; but none of those correspondents used the cable or telegraph. The Dutch East Indies had a very good newsagency at Batavia called Aneta, but again cable costs ruled that out for the *Straits Times*.

The front page was entirely given over to advertisements, as was the universal custom for conservative newspapers everywhere at that time (though no longer for the popular dailies in Fleet Street). The main news page was inside, in the centre of the paper opposite the leader page. There was a second page of local news — sport and the courts, mostly — and half a column of "Occasional Notes" (local paragraphs) and a "Social and Personal" corner on the leader page. The rest of the paper was made up of advertisements, with a few columns of reading matter, mostly clipped from other papers.

A regular item on the leader page was that hallmark of colonial society, the Government House Circular, which was followed with keen interest, as it named the ladies and gentlemen invited to lunch or dinner with the Governor and his lady, as well as noting His Excellency's other engagements. Another regular item in the news pages was the date and closing time of the P. &. O. Home mail, and the weekly tide-table — published because there were no swimming pools, and readers needed to know when it would be high tide at the Singapore Swimming Club (the European club) at Tanjong Rhu and elsewhere along the beaches.

The passenger list of every ship arriving from England was published in full, also that of the fortnightly P. & O. liner bound for Home. In that parochial European community people wanted to know who was going on leave, and who had come back.

There was no Business page. The daily rubber and tin prices, in London as well as Singapore, were prominently displayed, but there was no daily list of share prices, no reporting of commodity markets such as copra and Straits produce (largely jungle produce such as resins.) The three leading sharebroking firms in Singapore each produced a weekly report, and these were all published in full on the same day.

For other reading matter in the back pages the *Straits Times* was able to draw upon an old Eastern custom that is one of my most curious memories of journalism in Cecil Street. Tacked on to the last line of these columns would be the enigmatic word "Exchange". This meant that that item had been clipped from one of the many newspapers in the Far East, and also in Australia and New Zealand, with which the Straits Times exchanged free copies, on the understanding that they were able to use the *Straits Times* in the same way.

How long this had been going on in the *Straits Times* office we can see from a most interesting glimpse of it in operation in the 1850s which has been passed on to posterity by Sir Roland Braddell in his book *The Lights of Singapore,* and which he got from his father and grandfather.

The *Straits Times* office (the first in the paper's history, later burnt down) was then in Commercial Square (before it had been renamed Raffles Place.) This was what was known in the small European business community of that time as the *Straits Times* news-room.

"It was a large room, sixty feet by forty, and contained more than 100 newspapers from all parts of the globe, most of them exchanges, for the room was really the newspaper file-room of the editor of the *Straits Times*. It was also well supplied with prices current, maps, etc. and was the centre of the commercial part of the town. Officers of ships of war, commanders of merchant vessels and passengers who arrived by the many ships passing through were freely admitted, and from them the local inhabitants got much news, with the result that it was the most popular resort in the place."

On afternoons when there was nothing for me to report in town I would be handed a bundle of these papers to look through for "Exchange" clippings; and I would thus find myself looking at life as reflected in the Times of Ceylon, the Madras Mail, the Calcutta Statesman, the Rangoon Daily Times, three Hongkong dailies, the North China Daily News of Shanghai, the Manila Bulletin (a particularly lively paper then under American editorship), the Courier-Mail of Brisbane, the Sydney Bulletin, and Auckland and Wellington newspapers as well.

Actually, few of my selections were used and the Exchange custom was already dying out. The Exchange papers kept coming, but before long nobody bothered to open them at all. So I saw the last of a form of mutual aid in Eastern journalism that went back in Singapore a very long way — before any cable or other news services were available. Singapore had had cable communication with Britain, and thence with Europe and America, since 1871, when the last link in the chain, the cable to Madras, was opened. But as we have seen, it was of very little use to the newspapers for long after that.

6
The Governor's Book

DURING MY FIRST WEEK in the office — fresh from my Colchester bedsitter, as you might say — Snewin told me that I should sign the Governor's Book, the Colonial Secretary's Book and the G.O.C.'s Book. (The General Officer Commanding the military forces was always referred to by those initials).

The Governor's Book was kept in a sort of open sentry box outside the entrance gates of the Government House domain in Orchard Road. Every new member of the British community arriving from overseas was expected to sign this book, writing in it also the name of his firm or Government department or wherever he was employed.

No doubt His Excellency's secretary or A.D.C. listened in on the social grapevine to find out which of those names would rate an invitation to lunch or dinner at Government House; but the only result of signing the book that a newcomer of junior status like myself could expect would be an invitation to the King's Birthday garden party; and one duly arrived for me at the office during my first twelve months.

Signing the Governor's Book was mandatory, as an act of respect, if nothing else; but having done that, I had no wish to bring my arrival to the notice either of the Colonial Secretary at his residence in the Government House Domain or to the G.O.C. at Flagstaff House, which was two miles out of town at

Mount Rosie, off Chancery Lane; so I never knew what signing the books there might have led to. In the small European community of Snewin's younger days the full round of formalities was no doubt expected, but times had changed since the war, and I never heard anything more of it in the office.

On the King's Birthday the Governor and his lady entertained the European community (or rather, the British members of it) at a mammoth garden party in the grounds of Government House, and the upper crust of colonial society at a ball at Government House at night.

I cannot say whether the wharf and dockyard staff of the Harbour Board, or the warders at the Outram Road gaol, or the police officers below commissioned rank, were represented at the garden party; but certainly the European community as I knew it in Raffles Place and Empress Place would be at one or other of those two functions with their wives.

What was always referred to as "a European suit" had to be worn at the garden party; and as we sat the tables scattered over the lawns, eating sandwiches and cakes and icecream, it was a very hot and uncomfortable garb for a Singapore afternoon. Some of the leading Eurasian and Asiatic residents would be there too, similarly garbed.

The King's Birthday Ball was the event of the year for Singapore society, and it was a much more glamorous affair than the garden party, with officers of the garrison in dress uniform mingling with civilian residents in full evening dress. I never saw it myself, since the invitation for the *Straits Times* would have been restricted to the editor, and similarly at that level throughout the European community. I did not acquire the white-tie-and-tails uniform until later in my career, when I was assistant editor of the *Straits Times;* but that expensive suit made by a London tailor while on Home leave was worn only once, at one of the formal dinner parties at Government House, in what remained of peacetime life for Singapore.

So the King's Birthday in Singapore was celebrated as befitted the Raffles foundation and the capital of a British colony. But before all that there was the grand military parade in the morning on the Padang, watched by a huge concourse of people of all races. In addition to the regiment at Tanglin Barracks and other regular army units, the Singapore Volunteer Corps would be on parade — two European companies, the Eurasian company, the Straits Chinese company and the Malay company — together with detachments from the Sikh and Malay contingents of the Straits Settlements Police Force and from the Johore Military Forces. I have never forgotten the moment when the regiment in garrison was a Highland one, and the swing of the kilt as the battalion marched on to the padang in all the glorious colour of a Singapore morning.

But the King's Birthday Parade that I saw in my first year was the most interesting one of all, for it was the last held on the racecourse, the old racecourse that is now Farrer Park, and also the last time that the Sultan of Johore brought over under his personal command the full strength of the regiment that he maintained as his State troops. His Highness Sir Ibrahim was a fine figure of a man six feet tall (for there was Danish blood in him as well as Malay), and I can still see him galloping along that line of Malay infantry on his charger.

My one and only invitation to a Government House dinner party came much later between the wars — in 1937, when I was acting editor of the *Straits Times,* while the editor was on Home leave.

I remember the regimental band playing in the grounds outside the main entrance, and the Governor — Sir Shenton Thomas (who had come from one of the African colonies) — and Lady Thomas making their formal entrance into the drawing room where the guests were waiting. I also recall my alarm when H.E.'s private secretary came up to me and said: "Mr Peet, will you take Mrs ..... in to dinner". I did not even know the lady by sight, and was not sure I could find her among about twenty or thirty guests. Never had I performed this ritual before, but the lady obviously had, for she graciously took my right arm, and we joined the procession which marched into the dining-room. My wife was of course taken in by someone else.

What I chiefly remember about the whole occasion is the Ellenborough Plate, a magnificent dinner set of gold which had belonged to a former Viceroy of India and was set out along the long table. Did it survive the Japanese occupation? And where is it now?

It was naturally expected that guests invited to a formal dinner at Government House would make a point of being punctual, but when Noel Coward was invited he arrived twenty minutes late. The Governor was then Sir Cecil Clementi a scholarly, dignified and distinguished administrator who preceded Sir Shenton Thomas, and came from Hong Kong. Lady Clementi, justifiably irritated that Noel Coward had kept them and their guests waiting, let him know how she felt about it.

On his return to London Coward took his revenge by writing a musical comedy set in a colonial Government House, with the chorus singing a mocking refrain, "Menenti, Menenti" "Wait, Wait" — bazaar Malay. Sir Cecil Clementi was not a popular Governor and High Commissioner, and the malicious West End show was gleefully discussed at dinner parties in Singapore and Kuala Lumpur. To me it seemed a contemptible use of Noel Coward's talents, when he was in the wrong.

7
A Eurasian Goes "Home"

THE EDITORIAL STAFF of the *Straits Times* when I joined in 1923 consisted of the editor and two sub-editors — all of whom we have already met — and one reporter, a middle-aged Ceylonese Eurasian of British descent named A.F. Staples. He had been carrying on singlehanded for a long time, and greeted me with obvious thankfulness that some relief for him was now in sight.

Staples was a product of journalism in Colombo, at that time by far the best training ground for Asiatic newspaper men in the Far East. The only Asiatic journalists in the Straits Settlements and the F.M.S. able to hold their own with their European counterparts in my early days had all been trained in the English-language Press of Colombo, and the reason for that superior quality was the long tradition of sound English education under British administration in Ceylon. For the same cultural reason all the station-masters and clerical staff of the F.M.S. Railways came from the Jaffna Tamil province of Ceylon, as they had done since the construction of the first railways in Perak and Selangor.

The difference in this respect — pronunciation and vocabulary as well as written English — between Ceylonese and Indian immigrants of the clerical class in Malaya was remarkable. Perhaps Indian journalists trained in Calcutta, Madras and other centres did not find it worth while to take jobs in the Straits or the F.M.S., but, whatever the reason, I do not recall a single India-trained reporter on the Malayan Press between the wars.

Unfortunately Staples was handicapped by a dreadful inferiority complex, an inbuilt and pathetic lack of self-confidence that must have been the aftermath of his early life in Ceylon. His nervous, obsequious manner with European officials and business men was distressing to watch and listen to. Although he came from Ceylon he was more like the psychological wrecks sometimes produced by the British Raj among the subordinate Anglo-Indian class in India than the Ceylon burghers, as they were called — Eurasians of Dutch descent — some of whom did very well in planting and other employment in the F.M.S., or the Eurasians born and schooled in the Straits Settlements, who, generally speaking, were also of a sturdier type.

However, Staples was an experienced and reliable reporter, especially in the courts. He and I quickly settled down into our respective reporting rounds — both done by rickshaw — and all was going well until he startled me one morning with the news that he had been given four months "Home leave" and would be going to London, where he had two married daughters.

It was unheard of for anyone other than European staff to be given Home leave — home for Staples in this sense would have been Colombo — but this was a special reward for his services to the *Straits Times* during the 1914 - 1918 war, when the paper was shortstaffed and he must have been heavily overworked.

So Staples joyfully departed on a liner, and it was my turn to carry on singlehanded. Within a month, to my dismay, just turned twenty-one and a newcomer to Singapore, I found myself the only *Straits Times* reporter.

The *Free Press* had two reporters, a European and a Eurasian — a very good local boy trained in their office. The *Tribune* had only one reporter, a young local-born Indian; but they did not worry how much they missed, since they simply milked the morning paper for their own columns in the afternoon.

However, I was buoyed up by the thought that this was only for four months, and that Staples would soon be back to share the work again. But, alas, he came back a changed man. He had liked living in London so much that he could not settle again in Singapore. Family ties apart, I think he had found a new and happier way of life among those impersonal London crowds and kindly English folk — so much nicer in their own country than in a colonial environment — who cared nothing about the colour of his skin, who knew nothing of the social stigma that he had had to endure all those years as a Eurasian in the East.

Within weeks Staples was off again to London, this time for good. Some years later he wrote from London asking if he could come back to the *Straits Times,* but by then nobody in the office had ever heard of him, except me, and it was too late.

So once again I found myself the only *Straits Times* reporter, and that went on for another five or six months, in which I covered as best I could not only the courts and other jobs during the day, but often sport at the Cricket Club after work; and on Saturday afternoons — after a full working week — there was nearly always an important fixture on the Padang or at the new Anson Road sports stadium the first to be constructed in Singapore.

Towards the end of that first year another reporter arrived from England, a young fellow a bit older than myself. He obviously knew his job, and again I heaved a sigh of relief — but again I was to be disappointed.

The newcomer reported precisely one soccer match, and then withdrew to his boarding house, refusing to do any more work. He told me he was engaged to a girl in England and had been assured in London that his salary would be enough to get married in Singapore, but he had immediately discovered that he could not hope to do that during his first three years. So, he declared, the conditions of employment had been misrepresented, and he was entitled to break his legal agreement with the *Straits Times.*

This extraordinary situation went on for a week, with the newcomer still not coming to the office or doing any work, until it was ended by the management shipping him back Home. The company denied that there had been any misrepresentation, but the alternative would have been to let him become a destitute European beachcomber in Singapore, and a British firm could not afford to let that happen.

Perhaps also the editor and manager had heard that the National Union of Journalists was gaining ground in British newspaper offices, and a disgruntled recruit could have made trouble at Home.

Anyway, this reporter got a free trip out to Singapore and back, and did nothing for it, and presumably married his girl into the bargain. I never heard of that forceful character again until after the World War, when I came across his name in World Press News as the Manchester editor of one of the mass-circulation London dailies. He had risen to the top in Fleet Street.

Not long after that fiasco another junior reporter arrived from England who was quite content to work out his three-year agreement, and life became much easier for me.

I did not enjoy that first year on the *Straits Times* at all. On the contrary, I often felt badly overworked and overstrained. But perhaps it was an intensive course in local knowledge that was good for a young expatriate journalist just setting out on a career in Singapore, though I could not have appreciated it at the time.

8
Living In The Past

MY BOARDING HOUSE in Cavenagh Road was a most interesting place. That may seem odd, since the boarding house is a symbol of drab, prosaic living in English fiction. But not this one; for here we were living in the past (perhaps in more senses than the figurative one, for one night I awoke with a start to see two small children standing by my bed in the bright moonlight outside the mosquito net — a moment so real that I have never been able to reason myself out of it ever since).

It had been an imposing European private residence in the 19th Century, before it had come down in the world. It stood in a compound of four acres, with what had been the family's own mangosteen orchard still in the grounds. Even with the internal modifications that had been made, it was a house in which the most unimaginative of boarders could picture the spaciousness of domestic life, the life-style of the senior European residents of Singapore, in a bygone age.

So although I was at times a very bored young man in Mrs Matthews' well-run establishment, I was always conscious of emanations from the colonial past; and I knew that I would want to make a record of them in later years, when more modern ways of living had taken over.

Nobody knew the history of the old house when I lived there. But a clue to its period was the name of Cavenagh Road, which commemorated Colonel Orfeur Cavenagh, Governor of the Straits Settlements in 1861 - 67 and a veteran of the Indian Mutiny, the last of the Governors to come to Singapore from India. It must have been a new suburban road at that time, and the fact that the boarding house stood in such a large compound suggested that it was built at a time when Cavenagh Road was on the rural fringe of the town, when land was cheap there.

It looked exactly like the European compound houses to be seen in prints of early Singapore in Raffles Museum. In the 1920s, and for a long time afterwards, there were a number of large old houses in the same pattern still standing in the roads and lanes off Orchard Road, known to old residents as *Tanglin Kechil,* the European quarter before Tanglin was developed farther out. My boarding house was probably built in the 1880s, or even earlier; and the original owner was no doubt an affluent European merchant or professional man. By the standards of 1923, it was a huge house to have been occupied by one family.

It had no pretensions to architectural distinction, or even the picturesqueness usually associated with old colonial houses, being in fact much more interesting inside than outside. It was two-storeyed, much longer than it was wide, built of brick below and wood above, with verandahs the whole length of the house on two sides, on both the ground floor and the upper floor, and also at the back.

The most striking difference from modern design was the disproportionate height of the lower storey, which must have been twenty feet. But very high ceilings of ground-floor rooms, to keep them as cool as possible, were characteristic of old European houses everywhere in the tropical East. Even the ceilings of the bedrooms upstairs were higher than in modern homes.

The colour outside was the same faded yellow that one saw on old buildings everywhere in the Colony. For some reason the same kind of colourwash or plaster was always used on brickwork in the early days. There was not a glass window in the boarding house: only wooden shutters, slanted to let the breeze in.

The drive-in from the road ended in a massive portico, wide enough for shelter from rainy weather in the carriage days. The old stables were still to be seen in the courtyard at the back, but were now disused, since Mrs Matthews did not own a car. She had to send her house-boy down to Orchard Road to call a rickshaw whenever she required transport.

Above this portico was a lounge, open on three sides but roofed, which made a pleasant sitting-out place in the evenings. The house being built on a slope, one went up steps from the pillared porch to a paved hallway which gave access to both floors. On the right was a wide staircase curving in two flights of stairs to the floor above.

The principal rooms were on the ground floor, and this was always a cool, shadowy and restful refuge in the days when airconditioning was not even a dream of the future. Most of the ground floor was one huge room, with pillars down the middle supporting the upper floor, and several smaller rooms opening off it. It was paved with "Malacca tiles", the local name for a type of square flooring tile used in the early days which both in size and colour was like the paving slabs seen on garden paths and patios nowadays. One could see floors of this type hundreds of years old in Malacca and Penang, the colour toned down to a soft brick-red by age. And so it was in our boarding house.

It was a cool-looking floor too, for the Malacca tiles were not covered with matting anywhere. However, we never gave ourselves the pleasure of walking on it in bare feet, as I do now in my house in the heat of the Western Australian summer. Perhaps with good reason, for that floor was never washed or polished, so far as I know: only swept, and then with nothing more effective than a whisk broom. The electric vacuum, sweeper or polisher had not yet been invented for housewives.

This was our dining room, and I suppose it had always been that when it was a family residence. There was a long table at one end, with a *punkah* over it — still used — where Mrs Matthews took her meals. The boarders sat at small tables distributed through the room, two to a table. In our part of the dining room

— that is, nearly all of it — there was no *punkah*. Nor were there any electric fans, overhead or otherwise. The ceilings would have been too high for fans to be effective anyway. Yet as I remember that dining room during a Saturday or Sunday tiffin — the only days on which we had our midday meal there — it was always cool and comfortable.

Another thing in that dining room I should mention, because it was already a museum piece, though still in use, was a soapstone filter on a wooden stand, where one could get a drink of theoretically pure water. Memories of the days before Singapore had a modern water supply still lingered. The British engineers of the Municipality's water department scoffed at the notion that it was not safe to drink from the tap, but they had not convinced the public yet. I do not remember ever getting a drink from that filter, but I suppose that that was where the glass of water on the dinner table came from.

Another noteworthy object in the dining room — but not yet an archaic one — was a large wooden icebox, where the boarders could leave their own bottles if they wanted a cool drink. It was always a soft drink, or soda water for whisky — never beer, which seemed to be drunk nowhere except in the clubs.

Mrs Matthews' bedroom opened off the dining hall, and there was a son of about eighteen who also lived on the ground floor, but whom we rarely saw. Her best rooms for boarders were also on the ground floor. These were spacious enough for two men to share, with their own bathrooms — and that, as you will discover when we go upstairs, was an amenity well worth the higher rate charged for these rooms. It was also cooler on the ground floor during the day; and there were pleasant private verandahs, paved as in the dining hall with mellow Malacca tiles, with high brick pillars supporting the wooden verandahs overhead.

* * *

In front of the house a wide flight of paved steps led down to a grassy terrace and what had evidently been a very large and well-kept garden in the old days; but a bed or two of canna lilies and flowering creepers on low broken-down trellises were all that was left of it now. Below the terrace was the tennis court, on which we played occasionally at weekends; but the grass surface was in poor condition. If anybody wanted to use the court it was the *kebun's* (gardener) duty to turn out and put up the net — overtime for him, of course. He also looked after the potted plants which Mrs Matthews had about the house.

She had only one gardener for that huge compound, and the extraordinary thing about his job was the way he kept down the lallang, the tough local grass that will quickly grow into a dense matted cover two or three feet high if neglected. All this Indian gardener had was a sickle on a long handle which he swung over his head in a circular motion, moving slowly over the spacious grounds and chipping away at the lallang day after day. This was the universal method in suburban gardens, lawn mowers being then unknown except in extensive public grounds such as the Government House Domain or on golf courses.

For the tennis court there was a heavy iron roller, but in his singlehanded toil the *kebun* could have had neither the time nor energy to use it.

The rest of the four-acre compound was taken up with the mangosteen orchard. This delicious and beautiful fruit — sweet-sour sections like an orange, but snow-white and enclosed in a dark-red globe like a small cricket ball — is in a class by itself in Malayan fruits, so it is not surprising that a private mangosteen orchard should have been a common feature of the vast European compounds of the early days.

However the trees in this orchard were so old and neglected that they bore little fruit. I believe Mrs Matthews insisted on the *kebun* producing some for her table, but the pilfering house servants must have got most of it. When I explored the old orchard I found it swarming with mosquitoes. Below the orchard, at the foot of the hillside, was the railway from the terminus in Tank Road to Woodlands. In this locality it ran through a narrow valley, and when the railway was re-routed to the new terminus at Tanjong Pagar this part of the track became Clemenceau Avenue.

Dinner By Candlelight

DINNER WAS AT EIGHT O'CLOCK: the usual hour in European households, this late hour being fixed so as to allow for outdoor exercise in one form or another before sunset, and a bath and change afterwards.

The house-boys placed lighted candles on the little tables, enclosed in glass bowls to keep them from flickering in the breeze. The soft lighting faded into deep shadows in the corners and around the walls. There was subdued talk in the quietness — no distraction from radio or television in those days. The old house seemed to take on a different atmosphere, as if we were living in the past in that dining room. I remember that as the most pleasant time of all in our boarding house. But the dinner itself did not always contribute much to it.

It was always a five-course affair: soup, fish, meat, a sweet, cheese and biscuits, bread and butter. The thin soup, spinach or chicken, as prepared by a Chinese cook, was hardly worth drinking. The fish, bought fresh at the market that morning, and always served fried, was excellent.

The main course — Australian meat from the Cold Storage shop in Orchard Road, or sometimes tough roast fowl from the market — was served with a variety of vegetables, imported or local. There might be green peas from a tin, potatoes or carrots from Cold Storage, (only sweet potatoes were available in the market) locally grown greens such as spinach or runner beans (very poor and stringy), or egg-plant, or okra (locally called "lady's fingers"). These were bought by Mrs Matthews or her cook at the market every morning.

Salad vegetables such as green onions and lettuce were also available, but it was not safe to eat them without stringent precautions, because the Chinese market gardeners were still using human waste as manure, a practice which was not stopped until some years later.

The sweets produced by Cookie were plum duff, boiled jam pudding, pancakes — much too heavy for Europeans living in a perpetually hot climate — or a kind of blancmange served with dark syrup, which was not bad.

The cheese was always first-class: Edam cheese from Holland which came in large red globes, and so was known as "cannonball cheese", or Swiss gruyere, or gorgonzola. The butter was excellent too, if it came from Cold Storage; but if Mrs Matthews had been economising, it came out of a tin and was oily and unpalatable. The coffee was the strong, black, bitter native coffee from the Lampongs of Sumatra which Mrs Matthews bought at the market. You could buy American coffee in tins, but that would have been too expensive.

On the whole, except for the fried fish, the food was unappetising. The Chinese are a race of gourmets, from coolies to towkays (as one would have put it in those days), and Chinese cooks catering for their own people would carefully preserve and blend delicate and delicious flavours, also cook the local green vegetables just long enough to make them palatable without destroying the vitamins.

But when working for Europeans and trying to copy Western cuisine, the average Chinese cook spoilt the vegetables bought at Cold Storage and even those from the market, so that these were usually tasteless and overcooked. Cookie in our boarding house was no exception. His unsuitably heavy efforts with sweets were understandable, because sweets in the European sense played no part in a Chinese dinner, except perhaps the delicious tinned lychees from China to finish off a banquet.

On Sundays, however, it was all very different. Mrs Matthews and her cook put on a truly memorable curry tiffin, one in which she took a justifiable pride and which was in fact a local tradition for her, having been born and bred in Singapore.

With the curry — mutton, chicken, fish, prawns, or (the best of all to my taste) hardboiled ducks' eggs — came a dozen different side-dishes and savouries, some of them calculated to make the curry even hotter than it was already. As well as one or two dishes of curried vegetables, there would be an assortment of little dishes containing mango chutney from India, *ikan bilis* (tiny dried fish), red chilli sauce, a salty relish called "Bombay duck", shredded coconut, fried peanuts, chopped-up tomato and white onion, sliced banana, cucumber, and other bits and pieces I have probably forgotten. A marvellous mixture of flavours, but highly indigestible.

The curry was always followed in the old Straits tradition by a local sweet called Gula Melaka. This was really the Malay name for the native brown sugar, but in a curry tiffin it referred to the whole combination of sago and the syrup that one poured over it. The sago had a fresh flavour quite different from the product which my mother used to buy from the grocer to use in milk puddings, for it came from a palm which grows in Malayan swamps, and much more extensively in Borneo. The sugar from which the syrup was made also came from a palm. Malays tapped the sap of the wild sugar palm — or the brown sugar could also be made from the juice of the coconut palm.

Fortunately, when I was enjoying Gula Melaka at Mrs Matthews' table, I had not seen the crude process by which the pith of the sago palm was extracted to produce the article of commerce. Several years later, in a coastal swamp in Johore, I saw Chinese coolies treading it out with their bare feet in a long wooden trough filled with muddy water from a nearby creek, which served all human purposes for those who lived beside it.

Gula Melaka was delicious, but it was far too rich a sweet to eat on top of a big plateful of curry and rice with all the trimmings.

After tiffin one would lie down for a siesta and wake up from heavy sleep about four o'clock, feeling drugged in the afternoon heat.

It was several years before I brought myself to admit that the Sunday curry tiffin, an institution of European hospitality everywhere in Singapore at that time, could be a guzzle which stupefied the mind and meant saying goodbye to any worthwhile mental activity — to say nothing of spiritual observance — for the rest of the Sabbath. With temperance, however, and avoidance of most of those *sambals* (as the numerous relishes were called), it could still be enjoyed without ill-effects.

All this food for some twenty people — and, I should add, eggs and bacon, with toast, for breakfast every morning — came from a kitchen at the back which was part of the servants' quarters and connected with the main house by a long passageway, roofed for wet weather.

This was universal in all compound houses — that is to say: houses standing in their own grounds. I suppose the idea was partly to keep cooking smells out of the house; but in any case the oldfashioned breed of Chinese cook would never have fitted into a modern kitchen.

The main article of equipment he used was a squarish brick structure called a *dapor* (Malay word for kitchen), which burnt wood and was a sort of range of an Asiatic type; and he also used charcoal braziers to keep food hot.

As a boarder I would not have been expected to trespass in the servants' quarters, and I am here describing what I saw in my own household years later; but I am certain that Cookie in that boarding house, in preparing European meals for some twenty persons, was using equipment and methods that had not changed since the last century (although gas or electric stoves were already available in the shops).

* * *

The chap who shared my table in Mrs Matthews' dining room

— Frank Ziegele, an assistant with Brinkmann and Co. — deserves a place in this collection of Singaporeana for more reasons than one.

In the first place, he was one of the dwindling minority who still wore the Tutup. (Nothing to do with ballet, but the Malay word roughly meaning "closed"). This was the alternative form of European male dress, and it was a curious survival of the old way of life in British India, for it was a civilian garment of white cotton drill modelled on the military tunic.

The Tutup had a high stiff collar all around the neck, and was fastened by a row of large shiny metal buttons. These buttons were old Siamese coins, slightly concave, with a hole in the back. They were passed through the button-hole, and fastened with a safety-pin put through the little ring at the back. How these old Eastern coins came to be used in this odd Western adaptation, nobody knew. Ziegele's room-boy had to take out those metal buttons and transfer them to a fresh tutup every morning. The white drill trousers were the same as those worn with a jacket and tie.

The oldtimers of 1923 remembered when every man in the European community of Singapore, from Tuan Besar down to the newest-joined assistant, wore the Tutup; but by the time I arrived fashion had changed, and most men were wearing the Western-style white suits that Wing Loong had made for me.

However, the Tutup was still quite common enough to occasion no remark, and indeed it was a sort of recognised uniform for the European brokers in Raffles Place. The reason, as explained to me by one of their number, was that they were in and out of their offices so much during the day, and got so sweaty, that they needed a quick change, and the Tutup — worn with only a singlet underneath — lent itself more conveniently to that than a jacket worn with shirt and tie.

The Tutup looked hot, with that high collar, and buttoned-up neck to waist, but it evidently had its advantages.

I have to thank Ziegele, an extremely keen young business man, for whatever insight I got into what went on in the

European import and export firms. He was in the Produce Department of Brinkmann's, and when he was having his breakfast his mind was already on Change Alley, where he went every morning to bargain with the Chinese brokers for copra — and, I think, other things in the export trade collectively known as Straits Produce.

Change Alley was not then the tourist feature that it is now. (In fact, there was no organised tourist industry, though the occasional cruise ship gradually became more frequent between the wars.) Change Alley was then only what it was for my table-mate — the recognised meeting place for European buyers and Asiatic brokers. There were no stalls, so far as I recollect, or very few. Certainly it was much easier to walk through from Collyer Quay to Raffles Place than it is now, when the tourist has to push and shove his way through the congested narrow space between the stalls.

One or two mornings a week Ziegele would say that he had to go to "the godown" first. Brinkmann's were one of the last European firms to remain in their offices on Collyer Quay, but the old godown on the ground floor was now disused and their new one was somewhere in the hot and slummy district of Chinatown along the Singapore River. Ziegele would have to go there from Cavenagh Road by rickshaw. What he did there, I never knew.

On certain days in the month — once a fortnight, I think — Ziegele would be in a state of nervous tension at breakfast-time, impatient to jump into his rickshaw and be off, because it was "Mail Day" at the office, — the day on which the Home mail closed. Detailed reports and complete records had to be completed covering the previous fortnight in the Produce Department and all other departments in Brinkmann's, and in every similar import and export house in Singapore, for dispatch by mail to the Board of Directors in London or Manchester, to be digested by them a month later; and woe betide the Singapore staff if their principals at Home found fault with them.

Ziegele's father, a German merchant, had been in Singapore

before him, also with Brinkmann's, who were originally a German firm based in Manchester, but had become entirely British before the 1914 - 18 war. And now Frank Ziegele's son is in business there now, as I write — one of those family associations with the place through several generations that were not uncommon in the British community of those days (as in Malaya as a whole); but, I imagine, are rare today.

10

The Dutch Wife And The Jamban

UPSTAIRS IN THE HOUSE THERE was a wide but almost empty hall extending the whole length of the building, with five or six small bedrooms opening off it on either side. One could see where there had been very large family bedrooms in the old days, now partitioned off for boarders. Likewise, what had been continuous verandahs giving outside access to the bedrooms had been partitioned to give each boarder his own little verandah.

This hall or lounge between the rooms had a few pieces of rattan furniture and even a piano (though there was no-one able to play it in my time), but it was so stuffy and airless that it was never used — except once, when one of the boarders married a bride from Scotland, and Mrs Matthews gave a reception for them. Perhaps when the house was a family residence, and the whole upper floor was more open to the breeze, the area between the bedrooms was an upstairs lounge; but one wondered whether it could ever have been of much use.

On this floor, as below, there were no ceiling fans, and those rooms could be very hot during our weekends in the boarding house. A small movable fan of the table type available nowadays would have made all the difference, but this had apparently not yet come on the market. At any rate it was unknown to us.

My bedroom on this floor was deep but narrow, hardly more than a large cubicle. Suspended from the high ceiling by ropes was the wooden frame for the mosquito net, which was tucked up during the day and let down before dark.

On the bed was an object rarely seen nowadays: a long, thin bolster known as a "Dutch wife" (though presumably by some other tag in the Dutch East Indies). The sleeper was supposed to lie on his side, clasp the bolster to him and throw a leg over it for coolness — which will give the reader some idea of how hot it could be under the mosquito net at night. The "Dutch wife" was stuffed with kapok, a kind of cotton obtained from a tree which grows wild in Malaya, and it was used for that purpose because of its insulating property. The bolster was enclosed in a cotton slip like a pillow, and this was changed and sent to the dhoby once a week.

There was an overhead electric light in the bedroom — again, portable reading lamps seemed to be unknown at that time — but no bedlight, so one could not read in bed.

Within a week or two of my arrival I was lying on that bed sweating and aching for several days with dengue fever, known as "breakbone fever" in some tropical countries because of the intense muscular pain that one has with it down the back and legs. Everybody in the European community got dengue shortly after they arrived in those days, but usually never again, as was the case with me. It was carried by mosquitoes, but not the malarial species.

The bedroom furniture was a wash-stand with china basin and ewer, a small table and chair, and an almeirah (the local word for wardrobe, as it had been in Portuguese Malacca). In that almeirah, on the clean white suits and underwear, there might be the germs of a most unpleasant infection known as "dhoby itch", because it was believed to be contracted from clothing brought back by the dhoby. It was a form of ringworm, and it affected only one part of the body, the groin. The treatment was to paint the reddened semi-circle with a nasty preparation from the chemist, and that very private application required willpower, for it was quite painful. One's skin seemed to become immune to "dhoby itch" sooner or later; but newcomers — of both sexes —

almost always got it.

My bedroom had high wooden double doors — never closed — and also half-length swing doors, open top and bottom, for coolness. On the verandah outside was a rattan screen or blind, which was usually kept rolled up. This was called a *chick*, but where that word came from I never found out. It was there mainly as a protection against the sudden squalls of driving rain called "sumatras", because they blew up from the west, from Sumatra across the Straits of Malacca.

A sumatra could come up very quickly, with no warning except a sudden roaring in the trees outside; and if a squall hit the boarding house in the middle of the night there would be a wild leap by a sleep-dazed figure from under the mosquito net to unloose the cord that let down the *chick*. Sometimes during the north-east monsoon from December to February, the nearest that Singapore ever gets to a winter, the wooden shutters of the bedroom window would have to be closed as well.

Under my bed — under all the beds on that floor — was a wooden case of bottled drinks — lemonade, tonic, ginger ale, etc., ordered from the Fraser and Neave factory in Tanjong Pagar Road.

Never in that hot and sweaty climate did we drink water. I have always suspected that the frequent consumption of fizzy drinks must have had something to do with the constipation that was so common in those days. There was an assortment of laxatives and purgatives in every one of those bachelor bedrooms.

But the main cause of this malfunctioning was undoubtedly the unbalanced menu in the dining room downstairs — too much protein and carbohydrate, not enough fruit and vegetables. Moreover, we all ate too much, even for young fit men playing vigorous games at the Cricket Club, too much for a perpetually hot and enervating climate. I think most Europeans over-ate in those days.

I used to supplement my boarding-house diet with local fruit brought from the Chinese shops in Orchard Road and consumed in my room. Nevertheless, I developed what the doctors called "a growling appendix", and was operated on for it during that first three-year agreement. In later years, after I married, we were able to make a more rational adaptation to the climate. However, psychological reactions to the sanitary facilities at my boarding house must have had something to do with those troubles as well.

* * *

At the back was the worst feature of the boarding-house, the bathrooms. These were built out over a high verandah, with back stairs for the Tamil coolies whose job it was to carry bath water and empty human wastes. Each bathroom had a waist-high earthenware receptacle known as a "Shanghai jar". This was filled with water every day, and you dashed it over your body with a tin dipper.

Those bathrooms were dark and dank, and the cement floor was always slippery, an ideal breeding ground for the fungus known as "Singapore foot". There was a lattice board on which to stand in the hope of escaping this infection; and talcum powder was always used on the feet after bathing; but in spite of all precautions one was hardly ever free from the itching between the toes caused by "Singapore foot", and if neglected, it could be more serious than that.

In a corner of the bathroom stood the *jamban* (a Malay word for privy, not to be confused with *jambang* meaning flowerpot). This was a conical enamel bucket in a metal frame, with a wooden seat.

With about a dozen boarders on that upper floor, and the *jambans* emptied by the Municipality's nightsoil coolies once every 24 hours, the sanitary arrangements were indescribably primitive and disgusting (most of all during public holidays, particularly the Hindu New Year festival of Thaipusam, when the noisome nightsoil truck might not make its usual daily round.)

It was by far the worst part of boarding-house life at that time and not only in our boarding house, but in all other similar establishments and nearly every private suburban house in Singapore, except in the select European residential quarter of Tanglin. "There's something in that — as the monkey said when he put his paw in the *jamban*" ..... does anybody except me remember that old Singapore joke today!

Washing and cleansing the *jambans* was done by a lowly member of the Chinese domestic staff known as the *tukan ayer*. These Malay words mean water carrier, and in the early days of Singapore, before there was a piped water supply, that literally was the *tukan ayer's* job, as water had to be brought for the household from a well. (Several of these old private wells were uncovered in the heart of Chinatown during slum clearance work in early years.) The *tukan ayer* in Mrs Matthew's establishment still had to carry water, up the back stairs from an outdoor tap to fill the Shanghai jars in the four bathrooms; but he had the *jamban* job as well.

* * *

Every boarder was expected to employ and pay a personal house-boy, whose duties were to keep his room clean and tidy, wait on him at table, and perform such other services as he required. However, Mrs Matthews arranged for me to share a boy with the young Scotsman in the next room — an economy for which I was thankful at that time.

My boy was a Javanese, the only one of the house-boys who was not Chinese. The Chinese were all Hylams, as immigrants from the island of Hainan were called. Their language was quite different from that of half a dozen languages of South China spoken in Singapore. The servants in European houses, and also in the hotels, were always Hylams; and it was not without significance that they were the first converts that the newly founded Communist Party of China made in Singapore.

My boy's name was Zain (only a phonetic guess, as I never saw it written), and as a Muslim he wore the batik headdress of Java, quite different from the *songkok* or round cap of the Malays. He also wore the sarong, whereas the Hylam servants were in white trousers. I paid him eight dollars a month, and my neighbour the same.

Zain lived at the back somewhere, in the servants' quarters detached from the house; how he lived there, whether he got free board and lodging from Mrs Matthews with the other servants, or whether they had to pay Cookie something out of their low wages for their food, I never knew; and I am sorry to have to add that it is only now, in old age, that it has ever occured to me to ask that question.

About 6.30 a.m. Zain would appear in my room with early-morning tea. No such pleasant custom had ever come my way before (if one discounts the stewed brew in a thick mug which the steward brought to my cabin on the *Glaucus*), but it was universal in the European homes, boarding houses and hotels of Singapore. In a huge hotel like Raffles, for example, this service was rendered to all guests on all three floors as a matter of course, and — what will astonish people who know the costs of tourist travel today — at no extra charge.

In that hot, humid and evergreen land of eternal summer the most beautiful time of day is the cool hour after dawn, especially if the window of your bedroom is open to the scents and birdsong of the garden (as it cannot be in the airconditioned boxes of today); and that is how and when my day in the boarding house began.

It was not just a "cupper", as Australians would say, but a tray on which there was a little pot of tea, with sugar and milk, always a piece of fresh local fruit — papaya, banana or pomelo (the ancestor of the grapefruit) — and two thin slices of bread and butter. The tea was very necessary to wake you up from a night under the mosquito net; and there is no more cleansing a fruit to start the day than freshly cut papaya with a slice of lime (the little local limes which in Singapore are a substitute for expensive imported lemons). However, one certainly did not need the bread and butter, with breakfast coming up an hour later; and I think that must have been a survival of more leisurely days when

Europeans used to go riding or walking in the suburbs before breakfast. We had to get ready for office at a brisker pace.

After setting down the tray Zain would go to the almeirah and put out for me a clean white suit, shirt, vest and white cotton socks. Big detachable mother-of-pearl buttons were worn with the jacket, but as these would have been smashed by the methods used in the dhoby's small establishment — only the ground floor of a shophouse — Zain had to take out the buttons from yesterday's soiled suit and put them on the fresh one, fastening them with a pin at the back.

Then Zain would go back downstairs with my shoes, polish them and leave them outside my door. Having been brought up to make my own bed and clean my own shoes, I never felt quite at ease with this Eastern valet service; but one had to go along with it.

At breakfast Zain would appear from behind a screen in the dining hall and serve me. After that, I suppose he went back upstairs to sweep and dust my room and tuck up the mosquito net for the day. In the late afternoon, before dark, he let it down again. And at dinner-time he would be on duty again. But before that I might need hot water for a bath — not always, but on a rainy and chilly evening, when the water in the Shanghai jar would be too cold. I would then go to my verandah and bellow "Zain, *ayer panas*", and he would bring a bucket of hot water up the back stairs. (As far as I know, he understood no English at all).

Zain was a dignified, patient, impassive figure, with much better manners than my own; and what he had to endure from my fumbling use of a few Malay words from an elementary phrase-book, and my impatience and bad temper when he failed to understand, will not bear thinking of now. Poor chap, I heard that he had died of tuberculosis after I moved elsewhere, and for all I know he may have been ill when he was waiting on me.

Simply because Zain was Javanese, I was the only boarder who knew his room-boy's name, so far as I know. All the other men just shouted "Boy", and one of the Hylam boys (not necessarily his own) would come upstairs. Presumably they took it in turn.

There was no such thing as a Saturday afternoon off or a Sunday off for Zain all the year round, except at his own Muslim New Year, the Hari Raya holiday. For the Hylam boys the only holiday was at Chinese New Year. They were, however, much less tied to their work than their counterparts in European married households, as we were away all day during the week, and never called for a room-boy after dinner, whereas in a married household they might be on duty till late at night if the employer had dinner guests.

11
The Rickshaw Procession

AFTER BREAKFAST there would be half a dozen rickshaws waiting in the drive outside the portico, of all the fifteen or sixteen boarders — all working for British firms — only one owned a car, and one had a motor cycle. Two business men, slightly older and more affluent than the rest of us, went to office in an old secondhand car; and four young men who worked for Fraser and Neave shared a taxi. But for the majority, it was a rickshaw on monthly contract.

It was always a pleasant moment when I mounted my rickshaw for the ride to the office. Cavenagh Road at that time was a narrow and quiet suburban road, and, like all the roads in the older residential localities, was lined on both sides with magnificent old shade trees — bare trunks like masts rising 150 feet to the canopy of foliage which met overhead. These were in fact hardwood trees from the Malayan jungle, and one saw them in that suburban setting in their native jungle height and shape because they soared high above the telephone wires and so did not have to be lopped and mutilated.

Cavenagh Road — again like all the suburban roads — was surfaced with laterite (an ironstone gravel), contrasting with the green pillared nave overhead. Only the main roads leading into town had been asphalted at that time. The rickshaw had a collapsible canvas hood, so that when one emerged from this

THE RICKSHAW PROCESSION

shady side-road one did not have to ride in the full sun, which in Singapore is already hot by eight o'clock in the morning.

Debouching into Orchard Road, the main road from the European quarter of Tanglin to the down-town district, I joined a stream of other rickshaws, all going in the same direction, nearly all with European male passengers like myself.

The more senior Europeans lived farther out, where a car was essential. The younger men — and others who did not own a car — had to live within rickshaw distance of town. There were several boarding houses off Orchard Road in the area on Mount Elizabeth and other shady hill-top backwaters; but most of them were nearer town, behind the Chinese shophouses which lined Orchard Road, and extending back in a network of narrow streets to River Valley Road.

So out of the side-streets on that side of Orchard Road — Oxley Road and Oxley Rise and Kiliney Road — there flowed tributaries, as it were, to join the main rickshaw stream, until it became a truly extraordinary spectacle — hundreds of rickshaws in a column along Orchard Road as far as the eye could see, moving at a spanking pace towards the city, and each of them with a white-suited and topee'd passenger sitting under the hood — or, if he liked the sun, with the hood down — and, more often than not, reading the morning paper, the *Singapore Free Press,* quite oblivious of the traffic around him, or the human steed between the shafts.

Now and then a car from Tanglin would pass us, but I do not recall any impatient honking at the rickshaw pullers running two and three abreast. One-way streets were of course unheard of, but there would have been very little traffic going out of town at that time of the morning, so there was plenty of room for the traffic to spread out. There were no factories in the Tanglin area, so lorries would have been few and far between, and in fact I do not remember seeing them at all in my morning rides down Orchard Road.

What I do remember is the occasional bullock cart, with its thatched roof and Chinese coolie driver in his wide straw hat, lumbering along among the rickshaws with a load of produce from the countryside for Chinatown. So thin was the motor traffic that there was not a single policeman on point duty at any of the street junctions on the route to town.

Down we sped along Orchard Road and Stamford Road, then turned right into St. Andrew's Road, between the Cathedral and the Padang, and on into Empress Place. Here the rickshaw procession, swelled by another stream from the boarding houses in the River Valley Road district, and also by Eurasian and Asiatic employees of the European firms, banks and shops, suddenly intensified into the most extraordinary spectacle of all.

All that traffic had to cross the Singapore River by one bridge. Cavenagh Bridge was reserved for rickshaws and pedestrians, while Anderson Bridge, at the river mouth (built later, in 1910) was reserved for motor traffic and the electric trams from Collyer Quay. So Cavenagh Bridge at the morning peak-hour became a bottleneck, with an endless stream of rickshaw pullers and passengers speeding over it and fanning out into Raffles Place and Collyer Quay. In a census taken after the Great War 12,572 vehicles were counted crossing Cavenagh Bridge in a 12-hour period, all of them rickshaws except a few gharries. My own route beyond the bridge took me through Raffles Place and then another quarter of a mile down Cecil Street to the *Straits Times* office, on the verge of Chinatown.

I suppose that the rickshaw ride to the office became as monotonous as any other form of commuting, but there were certain mornings, and at a particular point on the route, when it became an unforgettably beautiful experience. This was when we turned the corner into St. Andrew's Road. At that time the Church of England cathedral (built by Indian convicts in the 1850s), still had its original weathered grey exterior, like a country church in England. The present dazzling white paint from ground to steeple, though regrettable to an oldtimer like me, was applied some years after the World War to preserve the stonework.

Moreover, the Cathedral compound — which has never quite

THE RICKSHAW PROCESSION

recovered from the emergency uses to which it was put during the siege of Singapore in February, 1942, and neglect in the subsequent British reoccupation — was like a green sanctuary itself, with venerable old trees and a wrought-iron fence all around it surmounting a low stone wall. This compound had been in fact preserved as an open space ever since East India Company times.

St. Andrew's Road was fringed on the cathedral side by huge old banyan trees which arched their great boughs over the road, and the road itself was a laterite red. On its other side was the grassy open expanse of the Padang; and beyond that, Connaught Drive was an avenue of flame-of-the-forest trees, planted on both sides. The flame-of-the-forest must surely be one of the most colourful street trees in the world. The blossom varies from deep-red to scarlet and orange — in fact, one of its names in India is the Gold Mohur tree — and the feathery foliage is beautiful too. (Botanically a Poinciana, it is a native of Madagascar.) Between and beyond those trees along Connaught Drive, one glimpsed the sparkling waters of the harbour.

Sitting behind my rickshaw puller under the blue dome and billowy white clouds of a sunny Singapore morning, with a heavenly silence and stillness all around me — for the motor traffic was all on the other side of the Padang, heading for Anderson Bridge — and looking at the old Cathedral and the green Padang and the ribbon of vivid colour along the Esplanade and at the waterfront beyond, I felt that that was indeed a lovely picture, the very heart of the old Settlement (as indeed it still is, though, alas, surrounded by swirling traffic now); and I felt too that that was a wonderful way to be going to the office and my prosaic rounds as a reporter. Such visionary moments did not come every day, but they remain one of the best of my Singapore memories.

That view across the Padang must have been even more beautiful earlier in the century, at the season of the year when the angsana trees which then lined Connaught Drive were in flower. The angsana is a much taller tree than the flame-of-the-forest, and it has a different blossom which fills the air with a heavy and delightful scent. Connaught Drive must have been indeed a lovely sight when the angsana blossom formed a yellow carpet on the roadway under the high green archway overhead. Unfortunately the trees became diseased and had to be cut down. The only survivors today are the three grand old angsanas in the riverside park beside Anderson Bridge.

The rickshaw itself was a colourful and bizarre detail in this picture. My puller was a splendidly fit young man, built like an athlete and looking like one, running on the flat road and the laterite gravel as if he really enjoyed it. He wore a pair of blue dungaree shorts, and nothing else, nothing on his feet either. His rickshaw was black and shining and polished till it shone in the sun, for these pullers — especially the younger men who had a regular contract or full-time employment (as some did, with well-to-do Chinese families) — took a pride in keeping their vehicles looking clean and smart.

There was another touch of bright colour, an orange-coloured feather duster which stood up in a metal socket where the shafts joined the bodywork in front of my seat. There was always a clean white cover on the seat as well; but that would have been provided by the Chinese business man from whom my puller hired his rickshaw.

I must add that on a wet morning — Singapore has many such, especially during the north-east monsoon, with a rainfall of 95 inches a year — the morning rickshaw procession was anything but a lively or animated spectacle.

For protection against the weather the rickshaw was provided with a canvas screen, theoretically waterproof, which stretched from the passenger's feet to his chest, and was fastened at the sides with snap-on buttons. But the canvas did not keep out driving rain, so one had to wear a macintosh, feeling unpleasantly damp and chilly at best and soaked at worst. And what of the unfortunate puller? Well, he might wear a sort of short canvas cloak over his shoulders on a really wet day, but most of the time he just ran bare to the waist in the rain.

THE RICKSHAW PROCESSION

From my seniors in the office I used to hear stories of rickshaw transport in their early days that astonished me. Snewin told me that while staying at Katong — then more of a seaside holiday resort than a residential suburb — he came to the office by rickshaw (about three miles as the roads were then). He also did this from another holiday bungalow at Pasir Panjang, which was even farther. It seems quite incredible that he should have endured that long, hot, tedious journey by rickshaw to work and back again; but gharries were the only other form of public transport, and they were comparatively expensive and not as ubiquitously available as rickshaws.

12
Conscience?

I REMEMBER MY MANAGER, himself one of the European oldtimers of Singapore, once remarking to me, "There are few pleasures in life to compare with riding behind a good puller on a sunny morning"; and he was quite right. But, you will ask, was not your enjoyment of those rides along St. Andrew's Road marred by qualms? Was it right for a healthy young Englishman to use another human being as if he were a draft animal?

Well, I often mused upon that question as I contemplated my puller's brawny back sweating in the heat and his muscular legs moving like pistons between the shafts. Was it really worse than letting a Chinese sampan man undertake the labour of rowing me out to a ship in the roads? Logically, perhaps not: yet one could not never quite rid oneself of the feeling that one occupation was compatible with human dignity, and the other was not. The association with a pony in the shafts was too insistent.

On the other hand, my puller needed a job and was obviously glad to have this one, and the freer and more independent life that it allowed, rather than working as a coolie in a godown or a rubber factory. And, after all, everywhere in Chinatown you would see Chinese coolies dragging heavy loads on the handcarts then in general use, and nobody ever questioned that.

What weighed with me chiefly, I think, was my manager's

contention that this was not a heavy physical strain for the puller. The rickshaw was so finely balanced on its high wheels and so light in construction that it almost ran of its own momentum on level ground — and most of the city was only just above sea level. On my route to the office there was not one uphill stretch. On the way back there was a rise in Cavenagh Road, but I always got out and walked there..... or am I being quite honest about that? Nearly always, anyway. But when one was tired and hot after an office day, one could be callous.

It was obvious that my rickshaw puller was a very fit and well-nourished young man, that his occupation was not doing him any harm. He could afford to feed himself well because with the steady monthly payment he got from me he was free to pick up extra fares as he pleased during the day — and rest between fares as well. These hire contracts were much sought after, and no doubt it was the younger and fitter men who won in the competition for them.

If the earnings were relatively good, the pullers could eat well at the street stalls. The Chinese working-class in general had a much better balanced diet than the Indian estate coolies and, even more so, the Malay peasantry — if it was only a bit of pork on the bowl of rice to provide the protein, and green vegetables to add the vitamins and mineral salts. My rickshaw puller certainly looked as fit as I was, if not more so — and the current popularity of jogging as I write in 1983 may help to explain why.

"The life of a rickshaw puller is only ten years" ... that was a saying commonly heard in Singapore in those days, and there must have been some foundation for it. But it was not supported by my own observations. I saw the same pullers on the same stand in Cecil Street, opposite our office, for at least ten years, and they looked as fit and cheerful as ever at the end of it. Several of my contemporaries who also used the rickshaw stands said the same.

It also used to be said that the rickshaw pullers were all opium smokers, and I believe there was no doubt about that, for the opium saloon was the only solace in a coolie's life.

But this is not the whole truth about the rickshaw industry, if one can call it an industry — and indeed it provided a living for thousands of Chinese immigrants. It is true that this vehicle ran easily and smoothly on level ground, but dragging a loaded rickshaw uphill was a very different matter — and there are hilly streets and roads in Singapore, plenty of them, behind the coastal plain. It was an everyday sight to see a puller toiling and sweating up a rise with a passenger, quite often two, and that was a sight I never did get used to.

Women used the rickshaw a great deal, especially to go to market (and marketing had to be a daily chore in the poorer Asiatic homes which had no icebox, to say nothing of a refrigerator). The puller was expected to take the housewife all the way home with her market produce, hill or no hill. In fact, I can still see Mrs Matthews laboriously coming back up the rise from the Orchard Road market on a Sunday morning in that way. It was unknown for a woman passenger to get out on a steep road, and few Asiatic male passengers would give the puller that relief either.

There were two types of rickshaw, the single and the double, and it was illegal to carry two passengers in a single-type rickshaw, but that regulation was never enforced. The double rickshaw, which was a less common type, and had a seat twice as wide, was still pulled by one man; and one would sometimes see a whole family, parents and children, packed into one of these wider rickshaws — and still sitting there when it came to a rise.

Most pathetic of all in the rickshaw industry was the old puller, who was no longer fit for the work but had to go on or starve (for there were no social welfare services in those days). One could tell the old puller by the tattered canvas shoes, or sometimes only a tied-on wrapping of sacking, which protected his feet. The younger pullers always ran barefoot in city streets and on suburban roads.

One of the first things I was told — by a young Eurasian reporter born in Singapore — was that when hiring a rickshaw I should always look first at the puller's feet, to avoid hiring one of those broken-down old men (who of course moved much more slowly than the average puller, and so were no good to an impatient passenger in a hurry to get somewhere).

It sounds heartless, and so it was, even if it was one of the facts of life. I confess with shame that I can remember one occasion when I acted upon that advice. I do not like to think now of the sadness I must have left behind when I glanced at the old coolie's sacking-covered feet, and turned away to look for a younger man.

The rickshaw puller did not own his own vehicle: he hired it by the day from a bigger operator. He was legally required to carry a printed fare card, which the passenger could demand to see (if he could make himself understood). This card, which was in a metal holder affixed to the bodywork in front of the passenger's seat, stated the legal fare per mile, or longer distances. It was only 10 cents for the first mile, but Europeans were expected to pay more, and local residents always did so. If the puller picked up a tourist who did not know this convention, he was quick to burst into loud and embarrassing protests.

The jinrickisha — to give it the name and spelling by which it was officially known — had been imported into Singapore from Shanghai in 1880. The industry was a monopoly of two clans of the Chinese immigrant population, the Henghwas and the Hockchieus (both from South China).

The pullers knew no English, and only a few words of bazaar Malay, so the non-Chinese passenger had to steer his puller, as it were, by shouting directions — *Kiri* (Left), *Kanan* (Right), *Trus* (Straight Ahead) or *Brenti* (Stop). A sightseeing traveller off a ship who could not give those directions was quite likely to find himself dumped at Raffles Hotel or at a brothel in some sinister sidestreet, those being the only likely destinations for a lost European stranger that the puzzled puller could think of.

My moralistic musings on the way to the office were comfortably academic, hypocritical, if you like, for they were beside the point, which was that there was no other way for me to get to and from work.

There was no bus service down Orchard Road, and I could not

yet afford a motor cycle. There was a tram service from Tank Road which would have deposited me in front of the office, but it would have been too far and too hot to walk down Orchard Road to the terminus in Tank Road at that time of the morning — I would have been in a muck sweat before I started work.

The tram route from Tank Road wound around the base of Fort Canning (now Central Park) along River Valley Road, up High Street and over Anderson Bridge, along Collyer Quay, and down Cecil Street to the terminus at Tanjong Pagar.

There were other tram routes through Chinatown and the inner suburbs, and I used the trams very occasionally when getting about the city during the day's work. There was a small compartment for first-class passengers behind the driver, and that, needless to say, was where I sat — usually in solitary state.

Cycling in the Essex countryside had been my chief recreation while living at Colchester, and during my first year on the *Straits Times* it occured to me that if I bought a bike and rode to work, I would enjoy that. But when I mentioned this idea to Hoppy at the sub-editors' table, I was advised against it immediately. Although he said no more, I sensed what was in his mind. Some of the Chinese clerks and Indian printers parked their bicycles in front of the office below, and it would not do for a member of the European staff to do likewise.

The only member of the European community whom I ever saw on a bicycle in those days was Bishop Ferguson-Davie, and I still have a clear mental picture of him riding one morning up Stamford Road from St. Andrew's Cathedral with his black cassock streaming behind him in the breeze. The bishop could afford that eccentricity, but in the European community as a whole there must have been an unspoken taboo against cycling.

The odd part of that recollection in the office is that on another occasion Ager told me about the European Cycling Club of which he was a founder member in his early days, and how he used to enjoy their Sunday-morning rides on the rural roads, then completely free from motor traffic. That was in the first decade of the century, and there had been some intangible shift of community attitudes since then.

If I had had a bike I could have filled in many empty and restless hours in the boarding house at weekends when there was nothing else to do. These colonial taboos seem so silly now that present day readers must be at a loss to understand them. They can in fact only be understood in terms of the fetish of White Prestige; and of all the echoes of life in the European community of Singapore between the wars, that is the most hollow, the most melancholy, of all.

13
The Last Of The Horse Age

THE HORSE AGE that the older residents had known in its heyday had finally petered out by the time I arrived (except for the gharries), but for several years I used to see a daily reminder of it in Orchard Road: a large noticeboard at the Tank Road corner which read "Abrams Horse Repository". The old stables and yard were still there, but had been disused long since.

"Daddy" Abrams, as he was generally known, was a well-known and horsey character in Singapore society around the turn of the century, especially on the Turf, and had formerly been in the service of the Sultan of Johore. European residents who did not have a carriage of their own used to hire one for special occasions at his stables, and bachelors hired hacks there for the Sunday-morning rides that were a popular form of exercise in those days.

When I saw that noticeboard "Daddy" Abrams' son had his own motor showroom elsewhere; and the valuable site at the Tank Road corner soon found a buyer for business development. Since the World War there has been redevelopment, and it is totally unrecognisable today.

One afternoon in 1925 I was riding along Connaught Drive in the traffic peak-hour — having graduated by then to a motor cycle — when I was startled to see, in the stream of cars leaving town after the office day, a smart little carriage coming along at a spanking pace in the opposite direction.

Two ponies abreast in the shafts were being driven by the Malay syce on his high seat in front; and, behind him, a pretty picture: two European ladies in the back seat with parasols to shelter them from the hot afternoon sun. Well ... neither was "European", strictly speaking. The elderly lady was Miss Sophia Blackmore, who came from Sydney and was the oldest missionary in the American Methodist Mission. After half a century in Singapore she saw no need for anything so newfangled as a car, and she still kept her pony carriage in the stables of the huge old colonial house on Mount Sophia, now owned by the mission, where she occupied the ground floor.

Her charming young companion on that drive was Elizabeth Lewis, an American girl who had taken a temporary teaching post in the Methodist Girls' School while passing through Singapore (and who shares this memory with me, as I write, in her home in Frederick, Maryland).

That was the last privately owned horse-carriage to be seen on the streets of Singapore. But in the 1930s, when I told that little story in the daily column I was writing for the *Straits Times,* several readers wrote in to say that they knew of Arab and other wealthy local families who still had their prewar carriages in the stables in the early 1920s. However, by 1925 the car had taken over for family use; and where those handsome equipages finished up, we shall never know.

Alas, not in Raffles Museum, and the nearest place to which the Singapore tourist could go to see their like today would be Perth, Western Australia, where a beautifully kept museum of every type of carriage is a rich man's hobby in the bush country of the Darling Range.

Gharries were still plying for hire in 1923, and the senior men in the European community had all used this form of transport as a matter of course in their younger years, but by 1923 they had their own cars, and the younger men used rickshaws around town and occasionally taxis for a longer journey.

There were a few taxis, old and shabby secondhand cars,

invariably driven by Sikhs, who had a monopoly of this business — and a bad reputation for truculence if the passenger insisted on paying according to the official rate card they were obliged to carry.

So when I questioned Ager about the gharries he said they were no longer used by Europeans — "but it's quite all right to ride in one ..." he added. Assured that this was not one of the things that were "not done" in my community, I did once use a gharry on a wet day, just for the experience, but found it a tedious and stuffy way of getting about.

The principal customers for the gharries by then appeared to be very conservative Indian, Chinese and Malay families whose womenfolk could thus venture on to the streets in the semi-purdah in which they still lived at home. No doubt the fact that they could get even closer privacy by pulling up the wooden shutter in the side-door — rather like the window in an oldfashioned railway carriage — was another asset in gharry transport from their point of view. But in fact the gharry was also already on its way out.

The author at the King's Birthday garden party in the grounds of Government House in 1938. Opposite him is the Chinese Consul-General and his wife. On his right are Dr Chen Su-Lan and his wife (active members of the Straits Chinese Methodist Church). Next to them is a lawyer named T.W. Ong, also a member of the Straits-born Chinese community of Singapore.

The old Seaview Hotel on the Katong coastline (now half a mile from the sea). The hotel is on the right, the modern bathing pavilion in front. On the diving board is Lora Buel, the author's wife.

The author, his wife and a friend.

The author's wife in Ginting Simpah, August 5, 1928.

The author's first car, a little two-seater Standard, with collapsible hood.

The Straits Times editorial staff in 1938. The author is on the right of the front row.

The editorial staff of the Straits Times in 1926, together with the general manager, photographed on the retirement of the editor, A.W. Still. Every member of it came from Britain. In the front row are A.P. Ager, A.W. Still and E.A. Snewin. In the back row are G.L. Peet (extreme left) and H.L. Hopkin (second from right).

Travel in the days of the passenger liners. Lora Buel on her way to Singapore.

The opening ceremony of Clifford Pier — June 3, 1933. The pier was named after the previous Governor, Sir Hugh Clifford and was officially opened by the then Governor, Sir Cecil Clementi.

Although the landscaped gardens around Government House were private, anyone could walk into the Domain through the gates. The author enjoyed many a quiet after-dinner stroll under the avenue of tembusu trees to which the Cavenagh Road gate gave access.

The Botanic Gardens were then as well-kept and managed as they are now but many familiar shrubs and flowers were absent then, having been imported only later. A band concert was given in the Gardens every month — the only occasion where the European and Eurasian communities were represented together.

Raffles Place — previously the heart of commercial Singapore. The older Europeans used to speak of it as "the Square", because it used to be Commercial Square. The name was changed in 1858. John Little, a department store still existent, was built in 1910 on the same site as its old store.

Woodlands railway station, in order to cross over to Johore Bahru one had to take the F.M.S. Railways passenger ferry from the jetty. The Johore Causeway was completed only in 1923.

With the advent of motor transport, the rural parts of the island became more accessible.

At the centre of the long facade of Raffles Institution fronting Beach Road, incorporated in the modern building, was part of the original school whose foundation stone was laid by Sir Stamford Raffles on 5 June 1823.

This photograph shows the first General Hospital at Outram Road, built in 1882. It was rebuilt in 1926. Conrad was once a patient here.

14
Ager's Punkah

IN THE LOBBY of the Singapore Cricket Club there was a green baize board sprinkled with visiting cards, reflecting an elaborate etiquette of Eastern society in which newly arrived bachelors and married people engaged, especially in the larger and more prestigious British firms and in the Government service; but I was happily spared this in the *Straits Times* office, perhaps because we were such a small European staff, and also because of the camaraderie that exists among newspaper men everywhere, even with a new colleague as junior as I was. Anyhow, my seniors evidently did not expect me to drop cards on their wives. Soon after I arrived they all entertained me very kindly in their homes, and four very different homes they were.

A Sunday curry tiffin with the general manager and his wife is a specially curious memory because that was the only time I ever saw the *punkah* in use in a European bungalow. The Agers lived in a *Straits Times* company house in Angullia Park, then a quiet backwater off Orchard Road. It had a pleasant verandah lounge in front, roofed for shade and shelter but open to the garden on three sides. But the dining room was only a narrow space in the centre of the house, with bedrooms opening off it on either side; and at that time of day, when we sat down at the table for tiffin, it was hot and airless, with no electric fan.

Over our heads, however, a *punkah* now began to wave slowly to and fro, animated by a cord which led behind a screen. The unseen operator was the Tamil *kebun*, and Mrs Ager told me he had the cord tied to his big toe; but I never found out whether that was just an old Singapore joke or whether it was true. The cord ran up to the ceiling and over a pulley.

The *punkah wallah* presumably got something for this overtime work, which was not just for guests but an everyday necessity at tiffin-time. Ager was one of the oldest European residents and his wife had been born there: they were just going on living as they had done in their early married life before the Great War.

By that time the electric ceiling fan had replaced the punkah everywhere else in European suburban living — or so I believed until in Perth in the 1970s I was surprised to learn from a lady who lived in the Straits Trading Company's housing estate at Bushey Park that the *punkah* in her house was in regular use up to 1930 (when she and her husband moved upcountry), and no doubt in the neighbouring company houses as well.

In the colonial mansion off Grange Road which was the official residence of the Straits Trading Company's general manager, and in which he entertained on a grand scale, the old *punkah* was brought back into use over the long dining table on those occasions as a curiosity to amuse his guests.

In front of the Agers' bungalow was the tennis court, which was in regular use every weekend in fine weather. Every European bungalow had its own court, and tennis parties were a favourite form of entertainment when, for most people, there was no golf course, — and for everybody — no swimming pool either. It was the *kebun's* job to put up and take down the net — but nothing extra for Saturday or Sunday work. Trade unionism was then unheard of in Singapore. The *kebun's* children or Cookie's, earned a few cents for acting as ball boys.

Ager played the violin, and he and three old friends, each of whom played a different instrument, met regularly at his house to play chamber music. In his early days he had conducted an orchestra which played for amateur dramatic productions. He told me once that music had been for him a great consolation.

"Well," he added, "not consolation, but..." I forget what word he substituted, but consolation was what he meant.

It was a hint of what life was like in Singapore after the turn of the century if you wanted something more than amateur theatricals and such professional entertainment as was provided by the occasional small touring company.

Mrs Ager had the local accent like her sister, Mrs Matthews, but I never knew whether she came of a Eurasian family or one in which the parents were both white, but had been unable to educate their children at Home, as sometimes happened.

Ager once told me indirectly how that marriage came about. Low pay, long periods between Home leave, the need to get out of bachelor boredom and have a home of your own ... so you married a girl of one of the local families. It must have worked very well when they were young together. A girl born and bred in Singapore knew much better than a bride from England how to manage the servants, plan good meals with what was available in the market, and make the husband's meagre salary go as far as possible — and she was probably much more contented.

The Agers did not go to the Tanglin Club, but they did not want to: they had their own friends, and were content with a quiet life. Mrs Ager was a kindly woman, with a fund of local knowledge, and she gave me helpful and motherly advice when I was new to the place. After Ager retired and settled in Guildford he used to go up to London to play in a good amateur orchestra until war broke out in 1939, and made up for what he must have missed during his long residence in Singapore.

The most formal of the office invitations soon after I arrived was naturally that from my new editor and his wife, but not so in the event, for I was the only guest, and what I chiefly remember is the homely atmosphere in which they entertained a nervous young man from Home that evening.

Mr and Mrs Still were then nearing the time for retirement from the East, having lived in India before they came to Singapore, and so were among the oldest European residents — also among the best known, for they must always have lived in the eye of the storm, as it were — so frequent were the controversies surrounding A.W. Still and the *Straits Times* (synonymous in the public mind during his editorship).

Their house, on a hillock off Chancery Lane, was quite a modest bungalow for anyone in Still's position, and he had converted a bedroom into a workshop for carpentry — his way of relaxing tensions after the office day, and a very unusual one in European suburban life at that time. Mrs Still told me they lived a quiet life, but they enjoyed the Saturday nights at the Tanglin Club, where everybody knew everybody else. "You don't meet Harbour Board types there," she said. "They stay on their side of the River."

How odd that that noisome creek should be a social frontier! But so it was — and in more ways than one, for it also divided Raffles Place from Empress Place, where the Europeans in Government service more or less kept to themselves in a separate social life of their own — naturally so, since most of them had lived upcountry in previous postings, and their experiences and background were quite different from those of the commercial community.

I learnt something else about the Tanglin Club. "Of course, nobody in trade ..." said Mrs Still. That meant exclusion of the managers of John Little's, Robinson's and Whiteaway Laidlaw's: three of the largest and most important businesses in Singapore. I, on the other hand, would be eligible for the Tanglin Club as a journalist, (or so I had been assured by Snewin in the office shortly after I arrived). But I had neither the money nor the inclination to test the truth of that, then or later.

So in that first and only evening in my editor's home I realised that the class consciousness of England had been imported into Singapore. However, I also realised that my host and hostess were personally very kindly people. They were just conventional British upper-class types (Scottish, actually); and the taboos of the Tanglin Club were identical with those they had first encountered in the even more caste-ridden Anglo-Indian society in which their Eastern lives had begun.

I got another insight into this white community of which I was now one of the most junior members when Snewin and his wife invited me to dinner at the Hotel de l'Europe, where they were living. "The Europe", as it was commonly referred to, was an old, very large and luxuriously appointed hotel, at the corner of St. Andrew's Road and High Street (where the High Court is now); and the Snewins had a suite there at the lower residential rate. Dinner in the spacious and dignified dining room downstairs, served silently and efficiently by the Chinese boys, would have impressed a much more sophisticated guest than I was.

We talked at dinner about Raffles Hotel, and the Snewins put me straight about that right away. "The Raffles", they said, although better known overseas, was definitely a second-rate place: all sorts of people went there. The Europe was the select hotel, the exclusive one for the best people in the European community, and it had stricter social barriers than the Raffles.

"If stengahs (Eurasians) come in here", said Snewin, "they are not actually refused admittance, but they are put off somewhere in a corner of the dining room, given slow service and cold food, and generally made to feel that they are not wanted. So they don't come again." Thus were the seeds of European prejudice against a whole community implanted in my mind in my first month.

Yet Snewin was a gentle and goodnatured man who, I am sure, would never have deliberately hurt anybody's feelings if he were meeting Eurasians in the flesh. His wife was not so likeable, a rather hard, aggressive woman; but in confirming her husband's view of the Raffles she was only saying what you might have heard from any of the European ladies who assumed that the Europe dining room and dance floor would be reserved for them and their kind on a Saturday night.

I met the Swiss manager of the Europe as a reporter later on, and he certainly ran the most arrogantly and unrepentantly exclusive hotel management in Singapore; but such freezing-out tactics were part of the technique of the professional restaurateur in many other cities, and this one knew what his patrons (mainly from Tanglin) wanted and expected.

The dinner invitation from Hoppy and his wife after my arrival is another interesting memory, but for a different reason. They were living in Meyer Mansions in North Bridge Road, a very large and rather shabby apartment block in an old-fashioned architectural style where flat life began in Singapore before the Great War. It was built by the Meyer family, one of several Jewish millionaire families in the business life of the city.

When I arrived in 1923 the only large modern block of flats built since the war was Amber Mansions, on the corner site in Orchard Road opposite the Presbyterian Church; but that was soon to be followed by others, notably Meyer Flats on the Katong coast.

Hoppy's wife was a member of the White Russian community which had fled from Russia after the Bolshevik revolution, and had since been making a precarious living in various ports along the China Coast: and he had met her in Bangkok when she was a member of a travelling concert party. So there was no social or racial snobbery in that home.

Hoppy and his wife were both interested in the theatre, in the touring stage and theatrical personalities who came to the Victoria Theatre, and they had a genuine love of music, both vocal and instrumental. Their life-style was quite different from that of my other European seniors in the office. But how Mrs Hoppy managed to fill in her time, living in that apartment with the traffic of North Bridge Road outside, I cannot imagine.

Ghosts Of Cecil Street

EUROPEAN BUSINESS DEVELOPMENT had extended by 1923 from the old city centre down Robinson Road, but had only just started along Cecil Street (both street names commemorating 19th century governors of the Colony).

Our side of Cecil Street was the frontier of Chinatown, as it were, in that part of the city, and the *Straits Times* was the only one of the old-established British firms that was so situated. There were one or two European and Indian firms on the other side of Cecil Street — in fact, one could gaze across the street at the attractive Eurasian girls working as typists on the corresponding floor of the Nestle Milk Company (which is as far as I ever got).

But for the most part Cecil Street was lined on both sides by Chinese tenement houses, three or four storeys high — picturesque facades with the family washing hanging on long poles projecting from the windows; but behind them, congested, terribly unhealthy interiors, mostly divided on the upper floors into dark and airless cubicles, the homes of the slum dwellers.

Cecil Street was situated on what had been a wide and deeply indented bay when Raffles landed, and for many years afterwards. The original curve of the bay could still be seen on the city map in the nearby Telok Ayer Street, a name which recalls the time when fresh water was obtained by seafarers on the beach there; and on that area stands the oldest Chinese temple in

Singapore (as it still does).

Ager told me that when the site for the *Straits Times* building was excavated about 1905 they found the remains of a stone quay, marking what was then the first of several successive reclamations pushing out into the bay. Looking seawards from our office verandah, therefore, it was all modern development out to the harbour front.

But at the back of our building, looking out into Stanley Street, it was pure Chinatown, with no Western intrusion whatsoever; and from there on it was a network of old Chinese streets as far as South Bridge Road and beyond.

On my first Sunday morning in Singapore — the day after I arrived — Ager had to go to the office and took me with him. While there he called me to the front verandah, saying there was something I ought to see. Indeed there was. What was a drab thoroughfare during the working week had become a corridor of gay colour and antique music. It was a Chinese funeral procession hundreds of yards long, with lovely silken banners and the clashing and clangour of Chinese musical instruments.

Most incongruously, however, it was led by a small Sikh band on a lorry, playing lively Western tunes more appropriate to a military parade than to that solemn occasion. The bandsmen had formerly served in the Indian Army or police bands, Ager told me. The family mourners in sackcloth walked behind the hearse, followed by the clansmen of the deceased, hundreds of them, bound by ties of Chinese social organisation and tradition of which the average European spectator was completely ignorant

The deceased had evidently been a wealthy and prominent man, judging by this display, for the funeral procession was very much a status symbol as well as public mourning. The nearest Chinese cemetery was miles away on the other side of town, so the marchers must have had a long, hot walk.

Such processions were a common sight in Singapore on Sunday mornings, when the streets were clear of traffic and the noisy trams were not running. In the longest and most lavish of these processions there might be two or three of the comic little

Western-type Sikh bands.

Apparently the China-born at that time, the immigrants who formed by far the larger part of the Chinese population, never saw that as a crude addition to the pageantry and the ritual they had brought from China. Nevertheless, the contrast between the sombre trappings of the European funeral and the spectacle of a Chinese community leader going to his last resting place with banners and music never ceased to impress me.

The old *Straits Times* office in Cecil Street — much altered a few years later, and enlarged by taking in the adjacent property — was of three storeys on a narrow frontage, built about 1906. A flight of wide wooden stairs led up to the editorial and advertising departments on the first floor. The floors were of wood everywhere, and were certainly never washed. Whether they were even swept I do not know, but I never saw anyone doing it, nor did I ever hear of office cleaners.

On the first floor, facing the street, the editor had a room to himself, with half-length swing doors for coolness, but separated from the sub-editors only by a partition open at the top, again for coolness. Snewin and Hoppy faced each other at a large table, and the two reporters (when there were two) had their desks in the same room.

Our room was open to the street. One stepped out on to a narrow verandah with overhead ceiling and concrete floor; and the noise of the old trams as they ground their way up Cecil Street along their almost worn-out iron rails from Tanjong Pagar was so deafening that if one were talking on the telephone, or indeed to anybody in the room, one would have to stop until the rattler had passed. There were ceiling fans in our room and the editor's room, and high ceilings, but they could still be hot workplaces, especially in the drowsy afternoons after tiffin, with heat and glare outside the verandah, when it was often a struggle to keep awake and get some work done.

The afternoon siesta — for which all shops and offices closed in French Indochina and the Dutch East Indies, except in the larger firms with international connections in Batavia (as it was then called) and Sourabaya — was unknown in Singapore or in business life upcountry.

On our verandah was a flush toilet — and that is worth mentioning, because it was not something that you took for granted in Singapore in 1923.

Sewerage in Singapore was delayed for many years because the civil engineers of the Municipality and the P.W.D. believed that a system with gravity flow could not be constructed on the coastal plain on which the old town and Chinatown were built (only a few feet above sea level in the adjacent harbour), but also because the Municipal Commissioners, most of whom were European residents, thought that European lavatories would prove unsuitable for the inhabitants of Chinatown.

Eventually consultants from overseas advised that sewerage was practicable with pumping stations, and their scheme was adopted; but construction did not begin until just before 1914, and progress was slowed during the war years.

By 1923 the central city area and Chinatown had been sewered. But the only suburb that had this amenity was Tanglin. The official explanation for thus favouring the European quarter was that there was a gravity flow down the Orchard Road Valley, but residents of less fashionable suburbs were cynical about that. However, the Municipal Commissioners must be given credit for the priority they gave to congested Chinatown.

Outside our room on the same floor was the advertising and accounts department, in which clerical staff were all Straits-born Chinese. The compositors on the top floor were all immigrants from South India. The proofreaders were all Indians too, but they were more likely to be local-born and locally educated — the sons or grandsons of Indian immigrants who had settled in Singapore. They had a sound knowledge of English and took a pride in their accurate and conscientious proofreading so it was rare to see a misprint in the *Straits Times*.

The skilled machine-hands who worked on the printing press in the basement were also South Indians — and here it is curious to recall that there was no European production manager to supervise those activities down below, as there was only a few years later. In 1923 the general manager did it all; and if anything went wrong with the flatbed press or the linotypes he called in the local firms that had supplied them, since these firms kept qualified men on their European staff to do any servicing that was required.

All the Chinese and Indian staff wore Western-type shirts and trousers, but the Malay *tambies* — office messengers and copy runners from the composing room upstairs — wore the sarong and Malay shirt.

This position of the Malays at the lowest level in the office was typical of the Singapore business world at the time. Everywhere in the city they had the poorest jobs, as *tambies* or syces for business men or as gardeners in the suburbs. If they did not work for wages they were fishermen, earning a bare living in the coastal kampongs.

There was, by the way, not a single girl in the *Straits Times* building. The telephone on the sub-editors' table may well have been the only one in the building. It was certainly the only one for both sub-editors and reporters, and the editor would not have a telephone on his desk. I can still see him coming into our room to take a call.

And, speaking of girls, what about the editor's secretary? ..... well, he didn't have one. And neither did the general manager. The editor dealt with his correspondence personally in longhand, but what the general manager did, I don't know.

A picturesque figure outside the *Straits Times* building whose very public life in Cecil Street always puzzled me was the Sikh *jaga*-watchman. His *charpoy*, a low wooden bed, (undoubtedly infested with bed bugs) was on the five-foot-way outside the entrance; and on this hot, dusty, ugly sidewalk he somehow managed to eat, sleep and perform his morning and evening ablutions. I imagine that by night the deep concrete drain in front was his latrine — as it was for hundreds of Chinese tenement dwellers living along Cecil Street.

The Sikh *jaga,* with a formidable cudgel handy, was to be seen outside every office in town, Chinese and Indian as well as European, and many shops as well. The Sikhs were employed for this job because they were twice as big and tall as the other Asiatic races.

16
Tek Wee And Baba Malay

THE CHIEF CLERK in the advertising department was a dignified figure named Lim Tek Wee, who had been with the *Straits Times* over 30 years. He was Ager's right-hand man. In fact, Ager told me that Tek Wee was the equivalent for the *Straits Times* management of the Chinese compradores employed by the British banks (enormously influential and powerful figures in their own right), in that his intimate knowledge of the Chinese business world — an entirely separate one from the European — enabled him to advise on the credit ratings of advertisers, customers for job printing, and so forth.

I am sure that that was so; but many years later — long after I had left the *Straits Times*, in fact — I learnt from my old friend Tan Ghee Tee, who was our chief clerk after the World War, but a junior clerk in those days, how very differently Tek Wee was viewed by the young men in that department whom he ruled with a rod of iron.

An hour after coming to work in the morning Tek Wee would hang his black silk coat over the back of his chair, as a sign that he was still around; but actually he then went back home, which was a simple matter for him, as his house was in Stanley Street, at the back of the office. During these and other absences the manager presumably supposed that Tek Wee was keeping up with his valuable contacts in Chinatown. However, after so many years with the *Straits Times,* Tek Wee no doubt felt that he was entitled to take things easily, and Ager certainly had no doubts about his value to the firm.

During my first year Ager took me with him to pay a ceremonial call on Tek Wee at Chinese New Year. His two-storey house — one of what would be called a terrace in England, but with no passage-way between the houses — had a very narrow frontage, with a tiny paved yard behind a high wall in front, but inside it obviously ran back a long way, with a courtyard in the middle to let in light.

As we crossed the street from the back of our building Ager told me that in the early years of the century Stanley Street had been one of the residential streets for well-to-do Chinese families, who then lived within walking distance of their business premises; but these families had gradually moved farther out of town, to new compound houses in less congested surroundings, and Tek Wee's house was the last that was kept in its original state. The front room for guests in which we were entertained had fine old blackwood furniture, with the family altar at the back.

The clerical staff in the advertising and accounts department all belonged to the same racial community, the Straits-born Chinese. They had been educated in the English-language schools of the Colony Government or the missions; indeed, they could not have got those jobs if they had not been able to read and write English. But, whenever I heard them talking among themselves at their desks in the office, they were invariably speaking Malay. This was not the pure Malay of the kampongs, but a local dialect known as Baba Malay, which had been brought to Singapore from Malacca in East India Company times.

Baba was a Malay word which in olden times could mean "any foreigner who was born in the country" (so Winstedt's dictionary says); but in Dutch and early British times in Malacca it had come to mean specifically the Straits-born Chinese living there, as distinct from the immigrants, the China-born. Having thus originated among a Malay community, Baba Malay was much **nearer the real thing than the bazaar Malay that was the** *lingua* *franca* of all races in Singapore in my day — and very much better than the pidgin Malay spoken by those European residents (myself included) whose contacts in their daily work were such that they did not have to learn this local lingo properly.

In their homes and family life, however, those clerks probably spoke Hokkien, Cantonese or another of the five or six Chinese dialects of South China that were represented in the Chinese population of Singapore. English was not yet the home language of any of the Chinese boys and girls in the English schools.

During my first year there was an office wedding, and that is one of my happiest memories of the *Straits Times* because it recalls a human relationship between the European and Asiatic staff that ceased to exist in later years between the wars.

The bridegroom was only a young clerk in the advertising department, but he belonged to a wealthy Straits-born Chinese family, and everything was done on a grand scale. The Europeans in the office were invited, and they all put in an appearance, except the editor.

With me, however, it was much more than that, for after the formal ceremonies I found myself put in the front seat of a car, with young Straits Chinese of my own age from the office in the backseat, and we careered up Orchard Road in a noisy and jolly procession of cars to another very large residence, where the festivities went on till late in the night. The Indian printers were represented too.

Away from our desks and our separate departments, we all seemed to be one office family that night.

* * *

The three senior Europeans in the *Straits Times* office followed the old custom of taking their tiffin there, as they had done since before the Great War. Their respective cars would bring them to Cecil Street at the start of the day's work, but the syces would then take the cars back for the Mems to use during the morning, for shopping and bridge parties or whatever. The editor's car would return about mid-day, and his syce would come up the stairs with a large wicker basket. Likewise, the manager's car.

The editor had his tiffin by himself on his private verandah, while Ager and Snewin — who brought his tiffin basket with him when he came to work — sat at a small table on our verandah (where at mid-day it was often uncomfortably hot). The contents of those baskets consisted of three layers: cold chicken or meat with salad: a sweet of some sort, and a plate of bread and butter, perhaps with cheese. There would also be a thermos flask.

During my first week or two in the boarding house Mrs Matthews told me that I too should have tiffin in the office, and she proceeded to buy for me a tiffin carrier. This was a gaudy enamelled metal contraption with three round containers which fitted into a frame, one above the other, and a carry handle at the top. This she filled with a similar three-course meal, and sent me off in my rickshaw after breakfast holding the tiffin carrier between my feet.

But I quickly realised that Mrs Matthews was behind the times, for I was the only one in the rickshaw procession down Orchard Road who was so furnished. Moreover, Ager and Snewin, who had known each other for many years, obviously preferred a quiet meal to themselves, without a young newcomer at the table. So I never used my tiffin carrier again, and went to the G.H. Cafe in Battery Road instead.

Before the Great War it had been the universal custom for European staff to take tiffin in the office; and it seems to have been anything but a leisurely break, judging by E.A. Brown's reminiscence in his book *Indiscreet Memories*:

> ..... *twenty minutes or so for tiffin — taken in the office — with the frequent risk of being called out to attend to a dealer, was the usual regime; and, mark you, everyone, from the Tuan Besar to newest-joined assistant, brought his tiffin down to office in a tiffin basket. The senior men would have*

their days to go over to the Singapore Club to tiffin and to meet others of their standing, but, generally speaking, Singapore in those days could be said to tiffin at its work.

The prewar tiffin rooms were still on the upper floors of the old godowns along Collyer Quay in 1923, but they had become disused, the younger men who had come out since the war preferring to go out for tiffin. One could get a monthly contract for tiffin in the European restaurant on the top floor of Robinson's or John Little's department store, and they served a substantial three-course lunch at a reduced rate. The G.H. Cafe always had curry and other local dishes on the menu. But all these places were open all day as cafes too.

There was no such thing as an office canteen in the *Straits Times* building for its Chinese clerical staff, its Indian printers and its Malay *tambies,* but there were food stalls in Cecil Street outside the office where they went at the tiffin break.

No such thing as an icebox for a cool drink after my rickshaw rounds either, or for the sub-editors. If we wanted a cool drink we would send a *tamby* down to one of those stalls, and he would bring back a glass of fizzy lemonade with a lump of ice floating in it. Or we could get a cup of strong native coffee, always sweetened with condensed milk. But hygiene at those street stalls would not bear thinking about. All cups and glasses were washed in the same bucket behind the stall, and whether the water in it was ever changed during the day ..... one never knew.

The Leader On The Poster

THE *STRAITS TIMES* MUST HAVE BEEN the only newspaper in the English-speaking world in 1923 that put the topic of its leading article on its poster every day. On the small old-fashioned poster that was displayed in Raffles Place and at the hotels there would be two or three news headings on the day, but the bottom line was always the heading on the leader.

In any newspaper today that would seem presumptuous, claiming too much for its opinions and for its own importance; but it was not so with the *Straits Times,* for the leader was the first thing that the readers looked at when they opened their paper — to see whether the editor was on the warpath or not.

The *Straits Times* leader was also the only one I have ever known that was identified in the public mind with the writer — not with the newspaper. "Still's leader" was how everybody referred to it when, as often happened, it was the conversation piece of the day in the European community. That is not a situation that would be approved in newspaper offices today — except where it related to personal bylines — but Still had been identified with the *Straits Times* since 1908, and his personality came through the anonymous print of the editorial column, though with the added weight of a responsible and reliable newspaper.

After tiffin on his verandah Still settled down to what was for him this by far the most important task of the day — and that always struck me as a remarkable feat of mental concentration, for the afternoon in that climate was the time when cerebral energies were at their lowest ebb for everybody else. It was Snewin's job to shield the editor from interruptions of every sort during that sacrosanct hour or two. Still wrote his leader in longhand and it was always set up in type by the same linotype operator, an elderly Indian who, I was assured, could not read English, yet made a faultless job of it.

When I joined the *Straits Times* Still was at the height of his reputation as an editor. People admired him as a fearless fighter, usually in a good cause from their point of view, and jokingly spoke of the *Straits Times* as "the Thunderer" — the nickname of *The Times* in Britain. In intellect and personality he stood out head and shoulders above anyone else in the Malayan Press at the time. He never went to the Singapore Club to drink stengahs with the Tuan Besars, but he was always remarkably well informed, at a time when what went on behind the scenes was much more important than the colonial facade. Still was also a natural statistician, and his lucid leaders on market trends in the Malayan rubber, tin and copra industries — and such arcane matters as Manchester piecegoods — commanded the respect of the business community. The manager of a French import and export firm in Singapore once told me that he had seen the rubber price go down half a cent — a significant shift in those days — after "Still's leader" had been read that afternoon in the offices around Raffles Place.

However, public life was quiet, dull and uneventful in the Colony and the F.M.S., and public opinion was only rarely stirred out of its habitual apathy and indifference over some controversy, or other. Writing six leaders a week, as Still had to do, it was not possible to find a local or Malayan topic every day. Three or four times a week he would have to look at the wider world for something to write about. In those days the editor of an Eastern newspaper was expected to be able to do that — to draw on his own reading or his own knowledge of world affairs, when there was no local topic for his leader column.

I recall, for example, a *Straits Times* leader on the fall of the historic Caliphate in Constantinople, based on nothing more than a single paragraph in the previous day's Reuter service. I recall, too, that first morning in Penang, ashore from the ship, studying the *Straits Echo* with professional interest at the old E. and O. Hotel, and how surprised I was to find that the leading article was in effect a review of a new book on British Prime Ministers.

A Singapore journalist would have to be very sure of himself, and of his backing in his own British community and his Board of Directors, to take on the Governor or the Colonial Secretary in those days, but they were both targets of Still's polemical battery during my first year or two.

Still had critics, even enemies, and he could let his crusading instinct run away with him. When I joined the *Straits Times* I was told that it had had to fight three libel actions since the war, and lost them all. The directors had let it be known that they wanted to pay out no more damages and legal costs. Public sympathy was strongly with Still in one of those cases, in which he accused the Singapore Cold Storage Company of exploiting its near monopoly in imported foodstuffs essential to the European diet (but not yet used in the Asiatic communities). The defence sent a commission to Perth, Western Australia, to inquire into costs, but failed to prove profiteering, and heavy damages were awarded.

It was the British rubber planters, however, who were Still's most devoted admirers. During the sudden and temporarily calamitous slump in rubber prices after the 1914 - 18 war Still had fought hard through the *Straits Times* for the restriction scheme that was already boosting prices back to profitability in 1923, after a year or two of sheer panic on the estates and the company board rooms. Still was strongly sympathetic with the planters, for he knew at first-hand how lonely and unhealthy their lives often were, lives in which marriage was impossible before the age of thirty or thereabouts because of low salaries and other bad conditions of service, particularly Home leave.

However, on the long run the rubber restriction scheme in Malays and Ceylon was Still's greatest mistake, for the Dutch East Indies got the benefit while refusing to come into it: and there was a huge increase in planting in smallholders in Sumatra and elsewhere while their counterparts in Malaya were not allowed any new planting at all.

18
A Fantastic Round

THE FANTASTIC MORNING ROUND which I had to do when I was the one and only *Straits Times* reporter, and which began when I hired a rickshaw from the stand in front of our office, is another illustration of the old journalism, and also another view of the Singapore of 1923 from an unusual angle.

My first call was at the Shipping Office, which was in an old building at the mouth of the Singapore River, facing Fullerton Road. It was also known as the Master Attendant's Office, and it must have been the same building in which an earlier Master Attendant gave Joseph Conrad his first command, the iron barque *Otago* (345 tons) then lying in the Menam River at Bangkok.

The senior Government officer with the curious old English title of Master Attendant was the head of the Marine Department, which controlled the harbour — the inner and outer roads (divided by the breakwater) off the Collyer Quay waterfront, and the junk anchorage off Rochore, the original port of Singapore in the days of sail, before the wharves and docks of Tanjong Pagar and Keppel Harbour were built. That part of the modern port was under a separate authority, the Singapore Harbour Board.

The Master Attendant was always a retired captain of the British merchant marine, a liner captain with the right social background to move in the higher ranks of the colonial hierarchy. The Senior Boarding Officer, also a master mariner but with local experience, was English, and the boarding officers under him were all members of the Portuguese Eurasian community, with names that were echoes of 16th Century Malacca.

The purpose of my call here was to make a list of all the ships, large or small, that had arrived or sailed within the last 24 hours, this being published in the *Straits Times* every day. But the Shipping Office was also the only source for news stories of the waterfront. The Eurasian boarding officers were friendly chaps who would give me a tip now and then.

Also in this office was the Marine Court, where the Master Attendant presided, and where the Court usher was a portly and genial Indian named Osman whom I got to know quite well.

Osman belonged to the Bombay Muslim community, and one day he was not there, having left to make the long and arduous pilgrimage to Mecca. That was before buses replaced camel caravans on the desert journey from the port of Jeddah. When he came back he was bitter about the extortion that the pilgrims from Malaya and Indonesia had to endure from the Arabs organising that transport. The hardships were too much for poor Osman, and he died soon after he came back to the Marine Court. The "pilgrim ships" — as they were called — were steamers specially fitted to carry thousands of deck passengers. They were owned by Alfred Holt and Co., and there were several sailings from Singapore during the pilgrim season every year.

The first story of the waterfront that I ever wrote for the *Straits Times* surely deserves a place in the maritime history of Singapore. The sailing ship *E.J. Spence,* an iron barque of 550 tons built at Sunderland, had arrived in harbour after an amazing voyage. She had been becalmed for two months off the Nicobars, and another 40 days drifting through the Straits of Malacca — a voyage of 112 days without calling at any port since leaving Mauritius. She had no auxiliary engine and no radio.

I took a motorboat from Johnston's Pier and went out to the ship. The master, an elderly and taciturn English mariner, seemed to think it was all in the day's work for him and his

Mauritian crew. He did admit, however, that at one time he had been "a bit worried" about shortage of water.

The *E.J. Spence* belonged to the last line of sailing ships to call regularly at Singapore, bringing ponies, sugar and other produce of Mauritius, and taking back Western imports from Singapore. This old trading link with Mauritius ended soon afterwards.

* * *

Leaving the Shipping Office, I leapt into my rickshaw again and my puller trotted across Cavenagh Bridge to the Supreme Court in Empress Place (the old Supreme Court which owes its preservation in the Singapore of today to its new role as Parliament House). There were always two judges sitting here. But this was only a preliminary inquiry to see what cases were coming on that day. Then back into my rickshaw again, down High Street and into South Bridge Road, to the Police Courts — a building which, like almost every other mentioned in these annals has long since been replaced by a more modern one.

Three police courts were in session all day long, each with a young European officer of the Malayan Civil Service sitting as Magistrate. There were local-born members of the Bar, Eurasian and Chinese, who had qualified at the Inns of Court or Oxford or Cambridge, but they were never appointed to the Bench.

The police inspectors who prosecuted in these courts were all European too, mostly recruited from the Royal Irish Constabulary, a fine service which then policed the whole of Ireland. There were no Eurasian or Asiatic inspectors in the Straits Settlements Police at that time.

This was a part of the working day that I hated, since a reporter was entirely dependent upon busy and impatient police officers or equally busy court ushers — Eurasian or Chinese — for tips on what cases would be coming up, and whether they would be worth reporting or not. It was only by cooperating with the Eurasian reporter from the *Free Press* and the local-born Indian reporter from the *Tribune* that I could get this job done at all.

A FANTASTIC ROUND

Having made the round of the courts, I went downstairs to send my handwritten gleanings to the office. Nowadays this would be done by telephone, with a fast copy-taker using a typewriter at the other end. In fact, I do not recall any public telephone boxes in Singapore at that time.

My copy-runner would be waiting for me in the crowded compound in front of the building. He was a *Straits Times tamby* with a bicycle, whose duty it was to meet me at the police courts — or the Supreme Court, if necessary — in the mornings, and take my copy back to the office.

My *tamby* was a young Indian and, as a sort of badge of office, he wore a red headdress. This had the advantage of enabling me to spot him quickly in the mob of various races always milling around the Police Courts compound. If I had to give him instructions, it was done in my pidgin Malay. After I had dispatched him with my police-courts copy I sometimes had to go back to the Supreme Court, a quarter of a mile away; and the *tamby* — whose name, I am ashamed to confess, I never knew — might have to meet me there again.

I have also to confess how I blotted my copy-book in an overwrought moment, not only in the figurative sense but in the journalistic sense as well, for it has to do with my Tamil copy-runner.

Back and forth like this between the Supreme Court and the Police Courts in the dense traffic of South Bridge Road, the slow pace of rickshaw transport could be maddening, with a deadline of 12.30 to meet. My *tamby,* however, naturally had no understanding of deadlines, and one very hot morning, in a moment of exasperation at his turning up late, I so far forgot myself as to give him a kick on the bottom: a public loss of face for him, as it happened in the crowded compound of the Police Courts Building, and a most disgraceful loss of self-control for me.

My *tamby* at once took off at top speed on his bicycle in the direction of the office; and when I got back there half an hour later the manager told me coldly that the *tamby* had complained to him about my behaviour, and, furthermore, was going to summons me for assault. For several mornings after that I saw him sitting at the back of one of the police courts, a forlorn figure waiting to find out what he had to do; but a poor man of the coolie class who could not afford a lawyer would not know how to go about summonsing a European.

My *tamby* finally gave it up and the affair blew over (with another copy runner assigned to me); but I am ashamed of it to this day. Such behaviour would have been generally frowned upon in the European community of that day, and Ager — without an actual reprimand — left me in no doubt that that was how he felt about it too.

If my morning finished at the police courts I would pick up another rickshaw there and go back to the office through Chinatown and so into Cecil Street. Was that not a remarkable tour of British and Chinese Singapore for a very young Englishman to be doing every morning! And at rickshaw pace too, an ideal way to observe the teeming life around you, whether you felt like it or not.

The best part of it was Cross Street and Upper Cross Street, which were then narrow corridors through the heart of Chinatown; and even though I was hot and sweaty after rushing hither and thither during the morning, and often feeling rather grubby and harassed as well, the interest I felt as I passed the five-foot way and the dark interior behind it in those Chinatown streets still comes back to me.

Another memory of those reporting rounds that may interest the Singapore journalists of today is of the small police station at the junction of Cecil Street and Tanjong Pagar Road then known as the Detective Station.

A swarm of plain-clothes detectives, Chinese and Indian but mainly the former, worked from there, and it was also the centre of a network of informers. These secret and mysterious activities were directed by the Chief Detective Inspector, and if I had heard during the morning of a gang robbery (the most common form of violent crime) it was to him that I had to go.

The Detective Station was in a way a symbol of its time, for the police force was still organised as it had been before the Great War, concerned only with crime, not with politics. There was as yet no Special Branch, so nobody in Singapore knew anything about the new Chinese Communist Party in Canton that was soon to send an emissary to Malaya; and as for symptoms of a new militant nationalism in Java — that was the business of the Dutch colonial administration, of no concern to their British counterparts across the Java Sea and the Straits of Malacca.

19
The Square

BEFORE WE LEAVE MY RICKSHAW ROUNDS let us take a look at other old buildings and streets that I was getting to know inside that morning orbit of mine; for although Empress Place was the heart of historic Singapore, Raffles Place and thereabouts was the heart of commercial Singapore, as it had been since the early years of the Settlement.

In the present-day National Museum on Stamford Road (Raffles Museum in my day) there is an old painting of Raffles Place done in 1904, and it looks almost the same as it did in 1923, except for the horse-drawn victorias waiting under the trees while the European ladies did their shopping.

The older European business and professional men whom one saw in Raffles Place still spoke of it as "the Square", because it used to be Commercial Square — but a very long time ago, for that name was changed by the Municipal Commissioners in 1858. When I went back in the 1970s I met one or two oldtimers of my day who were still giving themselves the nostalgic pleasure of calling it the Square.

The two department stores, John Little's and Robinson's, were on the same side of the Square, the latter still in its old red-fronted building seen in that painting, but John Little's had been built in 1910, on the same site as its old store. Both those names were echoes of early Singapore, for Robinson and Co. went back to 1857 and John Little and Co. to 1853, though the Little family had been prominent in the Settlement for many years before that, and one of its members actually arrived with Raffles.

The imposing bank buildings in Raffles Place, the Chartered Bank of India, Australia and China at one end and the Mercantile Bank of India at the other end, had been new in the first decade after the turn of the century. On the other side of Raffles Place, flanked on either side by very old shophouses, was a single modern building of four storeys occupied by European firms and professional men.

In Battery Road in 1923 there was a rickshaw stand in the middle of the narrow street — which shows you how little motor traffic was using it at that time (and of course one-way streets were unheard of). At the end of Battery Road was the other European department store, Whiteaway Laidlaw's, a name well-known all over British India.

Here the Hongkong and Shanghai Bank was in premises which it had built in 1901; and incorporated in the vaults of that bank were many of the rails laid for Singapore's first trams, by the Steam Tramway Company. The steam trains ran from 1886 to 1904, when the electrical trams of my day were introduced by a new local company. The small area between the bank and the G.P.O. was Fullerton Square — so named to commemorate Fort Fullerton, the first harbour defence work, which stood on the point between the River and the harbour and was finally demolished in 1889. Its cannons are also commemorated in the name of Battery Road.

Here was a group of buildings which were a survival of old Singapore, for the Chamber of Commerce and Exchange building was opened in 1879, and the G.P.O. probably about the same time (the Post Office having been moved from its original site beside the Town Hall on the other side of the river before that). This was the home of the Singapore Chamber of Commerce, a powerful body which, despite its comprehensive title, represented only the European firms, and predominantly the British ones. It was much more influential with the Colony

Government than the Chinese Chamber of Commerce — though the Chinese merchants could make the "Heaven-born" in the Colonial Secretariat and the Treasury in Empress Place sit up and take notice when they really wanted to, especially on any issue affecting trade or taxation. There was also the Indian Chamber of Commerce, but that was a comparatively minor body.

This building on the harbour front was also the home of the most exclusive of European institutions, the Singapore Club, which restricted its membership to the Tuan Besars, the managers of mercantile firms, and those in their offices who signed *per pro* (which meant one or two of the more senior men allowed to sign documents on behalf of the manager or managing director). There were also senior professional men, lawyers and others, in the limited membership.

Projecting from the first floor of the Singapore Club over Anderson Road was the verandah where the members used to enjoy sitting out over the waters of the harbour before Anderson Bridge was built in 1911 at the mouth of the river, and a new road along the front to connect with it — a pointer, by the way, to the traffic problem that the city was already having before the Great War, for the widening of Cavenagh Bridge was considered and rejected on the ground that it would be insufficient.

In the centre of Fullerton Square was a monument of early Singapore; an iron fountain erected as a memorial to Tan Kim Seng for his part in providing the city's first water supply. Tan Kim Seng, an outstanding leader of the Chinese community in his time and a philantropist (as so many of the self-made Chinese millionaires were) offered to finance a scheme to bring water from Bukit Timah in 1857, when all Singapore was dependent upon private wells, and these in the congested down-town areas were becoming more and more insanitary.

The donation offered, though a very generous one as money went in those days, was not nearly enough to pay for the Thomson Road reservoir, the first constructed to provide a piped water supply; but in 1882 the Municipal Commissioners erected this fountain near Johnston's Pier in honour of Tan Kim Seng. Alas, in 1923 the fountain never ran, the rusty ironwork was never painted; it held nothing but sand and rubbish; and I never saw anybody reading the inscription except me.

Around the fountain gharries waited for hire, the little Timor ponies munching from their nosebags and their syces sitting in the shade of the stunted trees. These used to be known as hack gharries. In the early years of the century there were private gharries as well, owned by people who could not afford a more elegant carriage; but they had completely gone out after the Great War. Those syces were all Boyanese. For some reason these immigrants from one small island off the east coast of Java specialised in pony management and transport. As cars and taxis became more numerous, they joined the ranks of the unemployed. (I would not have known that if I had not met one of them years later fishing off the rocks at Labrador one day because he had nothing else to do.)

Business had overflowed into Finlayson Green and down Robinson Road and Cecil Street before the Great War, but when I arrived nearly all the European firms and all the banks were concentrated in this small area in and around Raffles Place. The motor firms were in Orchard Road, but with that exception, and the Cold Storage Company's shop near the market, that main route to the European residential district was lined with shophouses on both sides as far as Grange Road.

20
Kling Street

THE MOST CURIOUS ECHO OF THE PAST — a past far beyond the British period — around Raffles Place in 1923 was Kling Street, a name which only the oldest residents of Singapore today will ever have heard, for it was changed soon afterwards to Chulia Street, its name today.

It had been Kling Street for a very long time, but after the Great War the leaders of the Indian community, and its English-educated members in general, felt that that street name had taken on a degrading connotation which it had not had in the past, since the only class of people now referred to as Klings were the Indian coolies, and they were the lowest of the low in the cosmopolitan population of Singapore.

They were the labourers seen working naked except for a G-string, their fine chocolate-brown bodies glistening and sweating in the heat, in the road gangs of the Municipality of the Public Works Department, or on the wharves at Tanjong Pagar, or on the European rubber estates that still existed on Singapore Island.

However, this social denigration to which the articulate Indians of 1923 were objecting had not always been so, either in modern times in the Straits Settlements or in the maritime history of the Straits of Malacca.

Kling Street was really a local name of great historical interest, for the origin of *Kling* was Kalinga, the ancient empire of southern India which had trading connections with the Malay Peninsula and Java and Sumatra in the early centuries of the Christian era, and was the first to plant higher civilisation in that region and in South-East Asia.

Those venturesome Indian traders (and Hindu and Buddhist priests with them) from the other side of the Bay of Bengal became known to the Malays as *Orang Kling*, because that was the only Indian race they knew, and the country of Kalinga the only part of India they had heard of.

In 19th-Century Singapore all Hindus from Madras and elsewhere in southern India — as distinct from the physically different Sikhs and the Muslims from Bombay — were known as Klings in the bazaar Malay which was the *lingua franca* of the place; but as time went on the term became restricted among English-speaking residents to the coolie class, Tamil or Telegu — though the Malays of the Peninsula still spoke of Indians of all classes from the Coromandel Coast as *Orang Kling*, and the Madras Presidency as *Negri Kling*.

Nevertheless, it remains an unsolved mystery why Kling Street should have got that name in the first place, for when Singapore was founded the immigrants from South India were known as Chulias to the first European merchants and officials, no doubt because they had all lived in India before moving to the Straits. That mine of local lore, Buckley's *Anecdotal History of Singapore,* says:

> "..... a petition was presented by the Chulias praying that a headman or Captain should be appointed for the mercantile and labouring classes. The lower classes of Chulias were prohibited from living in verandahs of houses or anywhere on the northern side of the town, and a Chulia kampong was marked out for them."

That petition was presented to Colonel Farquhar, whom

Raffles had left behind as Resident to administer his new Settlement, and Buckley says the site of the Chulia kampong was probably the modern Cross Street in Chinatown. Presumably the later European and Chinese settlers in Singapore heard the local kampong Malays referring to the Hindus as Klings, and took over that word from them.

Anyhow, in 1923 the Indian Association of Singapore was pressing for Kling Street to be given a less objectionable name, and one of the Indian members of the Municipal Commission, Dr H.S. Moonshi, was acting as their spokesman, though he himself was a Muslim. So the city fathers accepted his proposal that it should be re-named Chulia Street. But to both Europeans and local people the South Indian coolies were still known as Klings for a long time after that.

Chulia Street under its new name was still very much an Indian street, for it was the Street of the Chettiars, the chetties, as Singapore people always called them. These were a separate community of professional moneylenders from Madras, organised as family firms, and they were the only source of credit for people of too humble a status to go to the European or Chinese banks.

A Chinese clerk would go to them for a loan, especially for the weddings that were a crippling financial burden on office workers of his class; but the chetties were in business at higher levels than that, and Ager told me that the British bankers had a high respect for them as clients. He also told me that the finest mangoes you could ever hope to taste in Singapore were the baskets of choice fruit, specially imported from Madras, which the chetties presented to favoured clients at their Hindu New Year.

The chetties were quite different from any other types in the Indian community, for they wore a distinctive white costume, rather like the ordinary Indian dhoti but a more flowing and ampler garment; and they were always excessively and rather repellently corpulent, as if they ate too much and never took any exercise.

They had a Shylock reputation in enforcing payment on their promissory notes, whether always justified or not, I do not know — and a picture of the Asiatic business district behind Raffles Place which remains in my memory is of a chetty waiting ominously on the five-foot-way, accompanied by his tall Sikh bodyguard, for his prey to come out after work on pay-day.

Malacca Street, at the other end of Raffles Place, was another Indian business street; and it was there that I first caught a glimpse of the endless variety and fascination of Asiatic Singapore. One of the two out-of-work rubber planters who had been taken on by the *Straits Times* during the slump stayed on for a while after I arrived. His name was Calder, and on my first day in the office he invited me to go up to town with him for tiffin. So we took rickshaws in front of the office and went up to Raffles Place. On our way back Calder said he wanted to show me the shops of the Indian spice merchants, so he led me down Malacca Street; and sure enough, there came from those dark interiors strange scents that the Queen of Sheba might have known.

Calder had lived a lonely and isolated life on rubber estates, cut off from his own kind, literally on the edge of the jungle — for every rubber company was opening up new clearings as fast as possible during the boom before the Great War, and he had become rather queer and "jungly" himself. He had the public-school accent, but was definitely not one of the city types one saw in Raffles Place. Middle-aged bachelors in planting bungalows sometimes were a bit eccentric in those days. However, Calder went out of his way to befriend this self-conscious young Englishman fresh from Home, and that night after dinner he arrived at my boarding house in a hire-car — which I am sure he could ill afford — and took me for a drive to show me Chinese villages, Malay kampongs, rubber and coconut plantations on Singapore Island — though in the darkness I saw little of them. Before he moved to the city Calder had a Malay mistress, he told me that before he got this temporary job she had supported him during the slump in her kampong in rural Malacca.

Soon after I joined the staff Calder got a job at Kota Tinggi under the Stevenson rubber restriction scheme; and some years later, when I had found a new friend in a retired planter at Kota Tinggi, I heard what happened to him. He brought his mistress from Malacca to live with him in the Government resthouse, but Sultan Sir Ibrahim had a very good intelligence service of his own, and he did not approve of such arrangements when the European in question was a Government officer. One day the Sultan's Rolls Royce drove up to the resthouse, and that was the end of Calder. I never heard of him again, but I hope he got another planting job in the new rubber boom that was then under way.

21
The Old Godowns

THE OLDEST AND MOST PICTURESQUE PART of the business district around Raffles Place was Collyer Quay, and the continuous verandahs along the godowns above the five-foot-way were a remarkable feature of it.

The oldworld facade, in a uniform style all the way from Prince Street to Change Alley, had survived almost unchanged since it was built in 1860 - 64, when a whole new waterfront was constructed for the European merchants, who were finding the Singapore River too inconvenient and congested.

The very name was an historical echo too, since it commemorated Capt. Collyer, of the Madras Engineers, who as Chief Engineer of the civil Government constructed Fort Canning and these godowns as well, building first a new sea wall and filling in behind it with Indian convict labour.

The days of sail in Singapore harbour had already passed their peak when the construction of Collyer Quay began in 1860, for the Tanjong Pagar Dock Company was founded a year before that, and when its new wharf was opened in 1866 thirty-three steamers and twenty-eight sailing ships berthed alongside it.

But deep-sea shipping of both categories continued to use the outer roads long after that; and when I arrived there still were oldtimers in the European community who remembered when Collyer Quay really was a quay, with cargo from ships in the harbour being unloaded from lighters at high tide and taken into the godowns, or vice versa. The roadway along the waterfront was then only half the width it was in 1923.

Since the last of those 1860 godowns (formerly occupied by Paterson, Simons and Co.) was demolished in 1971, it may be interesting to record my recollections of them as they were in 1923. As one walked along the five-foot-way of Collyer Quay there was on the outer side a colonnade of high narrow arches, with the usual faded yellow plaster, and on the inner side thick brick walls of the same colour, with doorways opening into dark, almost windowless interiors.

In the old days the ground floor had been used for the storage of goods, with the offices above; but in the 1920s only the offices on the upper floor appeared to be used. Most of those firms were already waiting to move into modern office accommodation when it became available. Above the five-foot-way was a wide wooden verandah, with a balustrade on the outer side, which ran from one godown to the other; and oldtimers remembered when it had been possible to walk along this upper pathway to Change Alley, down to the ground there, and up again the other side. It was possible to walk an even longer distance than that, for the first-floor verandahs began in Prince Street at the junction with Raffles Place and continued to Collyer Quay.

In the days before office telephones a merchant who wanted to communicate with a firm farther along the street could save himself the trouble of going down the inside stairs of his godown, and up his neighbour's, by simply stepping out of his upper floor on to the verandah, walking along it, and stepping into the other office. No doubt also the shade and coolness of a wide verandah had something to do with it as well. The whole upper floor of these godowns was one open room for the European and clerical staff, with the manager behind a partition at the end.

De Souza Street, another of the old streets opening off Raffles Place with names redolent of local history, also had the overhead verandah on one side in 1923; but not D'Almeida Street, which had been modernised. An Eastern bank which few people have ever heard of today was the P. and O. Bank in its godown office in Prince Street — a name which comes back as an echo of the period in which that famous shipping line was paramount in the Far East.

Around the corner from Prince Street was the first building to break the low skyline of Collyer Quay: The Arcade, built in 1909 by the millionaire Arab family of Alkaff (from the Hadramaut coast of southern Arabia) on a site formerly owned by Guthrie and Co. Designed and coloured in the Moorish style, this tall building rose high above the old godowns. When it was first opened it actually had stables for horses and carriages on the ground floor. The only other modern building of the period before the Great War, so far as I can remember, was Winchester House, much lower than The Arcade and farther along Collyer Quay.

Only one new building on the Collyer Quay waterfront, and indeed in the entire downtown business district, had been constructed since the Great War ended five years before, and that was Ocean Building, on the corner site opposite Prince Street (occupied before the war by the famous German firm of Behn, Meyer and Co.).

During my first week on the *Straits Times* I reported the formal opening of that building, and it was one of the very rare occasions when the management went to the expense of making a half-tone block to go with a news story. The event was hailed as a heartening gesture of faith in the future of the port by Mansfield and Co., agents for the Blue Funnel Line and other associated shipping lines, since their new building had gone up during the postwar slump when everybody else in commercial and official Singapore was waiting for better times.

That first Ocean Building was of five storeys, and its design by the leading local architect of the day, said to be modelled on the famous Flatiron Building of New York, was much admired. Dwarfed though it is in recollection by the vastly impressive multi-storey home of Mansfield and Co. on that site today, and the imaginative and dramatic redevelopment of the whole

Collyer Quay frontage, it was in 1923 the first example of contemporary architecture that Singapore had seen.

The older men in the European commercial community remembered when nearly all the old-established import and export firms were on Collyer Quay. One of those oldtimers was E.A. Brown, who came out to Brinkmann and Co. as their Manchester piecegoods man in 1901, and who has left a record of those days in his book *Indiscreet Memories*. Brown's list of firms that were still in their godown offices in 1901 reads like a business directory of old-time Singapore. At the same time, in his book he passes on echoes of Collyer Quay as it was before his own time.

> *"The reason for this concentration on the front is obvious. In the old days, before the era of steam or electricity, firms had to be in a position from where they could scan the horizon for the arrival of ships; and when I came to Singapore every firm still had its telescope on the verandah, a relic of the days of sail. When steam and wireless came in, this necessity for a 'front seat' disappeared, and now (1932) there are very few of the old firms left in their original habitat."*

E.A. Brown was no writer, and there is too much social and snobbish trivia in his book, but one recollection of his early days moved him to write one of the finest and most memorable passages in the whole range of Singaporeana. Since his privately printed little book of memoirs has been long out of print, I cannot resist the pleasure of quoting his sketch of the annual arrival of the Bugis trading fleet as he saw it from Brinkmann's verandah on Collyer Quay.

> *"Picture to yourself a forest of sail appearing over the horizon away towards Rhio. Imagine the sea in that direction gradually becoming covered with small native schooners, 'Bugis boats' as they were*

THE OLD GODOWNS

called, until as far as the eye could see there seemed to be nothing but masts and sails. A wonderful sight it was to watch that fleet sail in — I have seen as many as three hundred boats — and how we used to watch for them! A tamby was always stationed on the verandah by the telescope to give the signal as soon as they appeared, and when they came to anchor off Tanjong Rhu and Clyde Terrace the harbour presented a most animated appearance.

"*And when it is remembered that those boats contained the fruits of a year's labour of the people of the Celebes and round about, and that they had come to barter that produce for the sarongs and prints, the pots and pans, the nails and hammers, and all the hundred and one things that made life worth living where they came from it can be imagined how the town hummed with activity.*

"*And remember also that what went on with the Bugis was going on every day with some other parts of the Eastern seas. Native craft of all kinds and from all places concentrated on Singapore. Here were the big steamers, ready to carry away the gathered produce to all parts of the Western world. Here were the great stores, full of things that the native wanted but could not make himself. Nowhere else in these Eastern waters at that time was there such a centre of trade and activity. Truly the name 'The Gateway of the East' was fully deserved.*"

That is just about as clear and simple an account of Singapore's entrepot trade as one could find, though by the time I arrived it had changed in some respects since Brown's early days in the piecegoods business. In particular, the new deepwater ports built by the Dutch in Java and Sumatra had proved formidable competitors in constricting Singapore's traditional role as the main focus of East-West exchange of goods and produce for the myriad islands of the Indonesian archipelago.

* * *

I cannot say that I have any nostalgic memories of Raffles Place, but I always enjoyed walking along the five-foot-way of Collyer Quay, with the harbour and its shipping seen through the arches — a completely open view along the sea wall then, of course — and passing the interesting old godowns.

Moreover, at the farther end one could escape from the city on to the rusting old iron structure known as Johnston's Pier. This was the only pier on the waterfront for people going to and from ships in the roads. It had no floating pontoon as a landing platform, so that one had to go down a flight of slippery iron steps washed by the tide to get into a sampan, and that could be hazardous.

Johnston's Pier was certainly obsolete, but it was my favourite spot during my reporting days around town. I used to enjoy looking at the lovely colour in the clear water (no talk of pollution then), the different races and costumes, the small ships of all shapes and sizes in the inner roads which traded to coasts and islands unknown to the city dweller, and the cluster of sampans that were always waiting for hire below the pier.

The sampan wallah rowed standing up facing his passenger and, as it were, pushing his oars backwards. This was the cheapest way to go out to a ship, but if it was anchored too far out for the slow progress of a sampan there were a few motorboats for hire. Another memory of Johnston's Pier is of the brown Brahminy kites soaring and swooping as they looked for garbage in the harbour. What has happened to these scavengers? They are rarely seen off Clifford Pier or anywhere else in the harbour now.

Although everybody was glad to see the last of Johnston's Pier when Clifford Pier was constructed farther along Collyer Quay in

1933, and so named by the then Governor, Sir Cecil Clementi, they were sorry to have to give up a name that was one of the landmarks of local history.

Johnston's Pier, although due for the scrapheap when I knew it, had seen some fine spectacles in its time, as it was the landing place for British Royalty visiting Singapore.

One such occasion which Ager recalled was watching the "Perak Lancers" escorting the Duke and Duchess of Cornwall when they landed at the old pier on their way to Australia in 1901. That was the personal bodyguard of the Sultan of Perak, lent by him for the Royal welcome. It was a mounted detachment of 20 Sikhs and an officer in scarlet uniform, selected from the Malay States Guides, a regiment of regular troops maintained by the F.M.S. Government at Taiping.

The original Johnston's Pier on this site belonged to one of the first British merchants to settle in Singapore after the Raffles foundation, A.L. Johnston. He came from India in 1820 and saw the place grow from "jungle to a thriving port" as he put it himself on his retirement to his native Scotland in the 1840s. A.L. Johnston had been a chief mate in the East India Company's fleet, and was a personal friend of Raffles.

22
Echoes In The Streets

SOME OF MY MOST interesting memories of Singapore in old age are of everyday sights that interest me in youth for a different reason — that reason being that even as a newcomer I realised that these were survivals of an earlier time that would soon disappear altogether, as in fact nearly all of them did during that first decade after the Great War.

For example, the picture in my mental album today of European ladies playing tennis and croquet in what was even then the improbable and unattractive locality of Dhoby Ghaut ..... The Ladies Lawn Tennis Club was still there in 1923, on its grassy strip of private land between Stamford Road and Bras Basah Road.

This was the most exclusive and snobbish meeting-place of colonial society in the early years of the century, and before that. To be elected a subscribing male member (without voting rights) by the ladies' committee was the hallmark of social distinction for any European bachelor.

The "Ladies Lawn", as it was always referred to, was also a citadel of stuffy etiquette. E.A. Brown recalls in his reminiscences that he was once severely ticked off for having lit his pipe while strolling across the courts one Saturday afternoon, when he thought there was no-one about, but when basilisk eyes were actually upon him from the club verandah.

In 1923 a few devoted members were still coming in from their suburban homes to play tennis and croquet as close to town as Dhoby Ghaut; and no doubt those living in Amber Mansions, the new block of flats opposite the Presbyterian Church, found it particularly convenient to cross the road for a game.

But by that time the Ladies Lawn was already on its last legs — if I may use such an indelicate metaphor. In the following year its courts were taken over by the Y.M.C.A. and its remaining lady members got their tennis at the Tanglin Club instead.

Unbelievable as this next memory of Stamford Road must seem to anyone who drives along that traffic artery today, it was there beyond the Ladies Lawn and the school playing field beyond it, one moonlight night, that I watched an old-world Malay ronggeng. It was being held in an open space on the other side of the monsoon drain that was one of the last relics of early Singapore, for it had been the courtyard of the old gaol, and, before that, part of the convict lines when Singapore was a penal station for India. The gaol had been disused since 1882, when the prisoners were transferred to the new Outram Road Prison; and at the time I am now recalling it was the headquarters of the Malay Volunteer Company.

Among the Malays facing the ronggeng girls in the dance movements, back and forth to the insistent rhythm of the gongs, were two Europeans whom I recognised as the magistrates whom I used to see on the Bench every day in the police courts, but whom I now saw in their other role as officers of the Malay Company. Because of their knowledge of the language, and experience in dealing with the Malay race, as members of the Malayan Civil Service, they were expected to take on those extra duties; but those two young men were also well qualified to do so by virtue of active service in the 1914 - 18 war.

Monotonous as the shuffling movements of the ronggeng dance were, and separated as the male dancers always were from the girls, it was to the Malay men of those times as sexually provocative as a burlesque is to Europeans, for their own womenfolk were kept in strict seclusion, and only prostitutes would venture upon the public dancing that the ronggeng girls performed. It was amusing to watch these normally reserved and dignified M.C.S. types surrendering more and more to the repressed eroticism of the ronggeng as the night wore on.

The high entrance archway of the old gaol, with its massive timber doors, faced Bras Basah Road; and round the corner, in the adjacent Victoria Street was a very large tree from the branches of which, so residents of that locality said, condemned criminals were publicly hanged in the old days.

That could have been true, for public executions took place outside the Outram Road Prison until the 1890s. In the *Straits Times* files I once came upon an appalling paragraph about two European ladies who went to see an execution there as a thrill before breakfast — and it was one in which the hangman botched his job, so death was plainly and visibly not instantaneous.

Another institution of a bygone age that one saw on the way to town in Stamford Road was the old Van Wijk Hotel, approached by a bridge over the deep monsoon drain. As its name implies, this was a Dutch hotel, with Javanese boys in their picturesque costume, and it catered chiefly for travellers to and from the Dutch East Indies; but the occasional British tourist liked its old-world atmosphere too. One of them was Somerset Maugham, whom I interviewed there once when he was on one of his leisurely wanderings off the beaten track in Malaya and the Dutch East Indies, with his male secretary and, so he told me, "a box of books". I have always remembered the charming courtesy and patience with which this famous author treated a young reporter who showed more interest in his enviable mode of Eastern travel than in his plays or books.

I remember Maugham telling me he had been staying in a Government resthouse in Kedah, and was on his way to some fascinating place in the Java Sea — I think Macassar. The beautifully kept passenger ships of the K.P.M. fleet sailed from Java to countless islands, and a traveller with leisure and money like Maugham could have a marvellous holiday exploring the East Indies on board them. My rival on the *Free Press,* who was interested in the London theatre, followed me to the Van Wijk and produced a much more competent interview.

A few years later Somerset Maugham might have struck unpleasantness in any resthouse in the Malay States, for he was intensely disliked after people thought they recognised the famous Proudlock murder case in Kuala Lumpur — the only one in Malayan history in which a white woman was sentenced to be hanged (but reprieved and banished by the Sultan of Selangor) — in one of his short stories. Maugham was accused in Hong Kong as well as Malaya of going around picking up bits of local scandal as material for his writing. He never bothered to refute any such crude assumptions about the way in which the literary imagination works on the raw material of human nature. (Conrad's novel *Almayer's Folly* is much closer to the personal realities of life up that river in Dutch East Borneo than any Somerset Maugham play or story). I do not think Maugham was ever as unpopular in Singapore as he was in the F.M.S.

The Van Wijk — which was the last building on the other side of Stamford Road before the canal passed under North Bridge Road — lasted a few more years before it was demolished, and the site used for the new secondary department of the adjacent Convent of the Holy Infant Jesus. Only then did a secret hitherto hidden in Lands Department files and some Singapore solicitor's safe come to light: the Convent had owned the old hotel for many years, and no doubt had put the income derived from its bar downstairs and bedrooms upstairs to very good use.

In all that historic strip of land between Stamford Road and Bras Basah Road, however, the most remarkable survival of early Singapore was at the very end of it. But it was invisible from the outside, and indeed unknown to most people.

At the centre of the long facade of Raffles Institution fronting Beach Road, incorporated in the modern building, was part of the original school whose foundation stone was laid by Sir Stamford Raffles on 5 June 1823. This was the building of which the *Singapore Free Press* (quoted by Buckley) said in 1832:

> "*The unfinished building, or rather ruin, so well known as the Singapore Institution, stands in a conspicuous situation at the head of Kampong Glam, on the town side fronting the sea-beach. To strangers it is often a matter of astonishment that a building in such an eligible site, and in the neighbourhood of so many respectable and new habitations, should be suffered to remain in its present delapidated condition..... For several years, it has been an eyesore to the inhabitants of the Settlement, from the desolate and neglected appearance of the building and premises; and latterly it has become a nuisance, in some degree, as it affords a convenient shelter for thieves.....*"

It remained a ruin until 1838, when it was repaired by public subscription and the school known as the Singapore Institution became a reality at last, though not as the multi-lingual college that Raffles proposed — a concept far too ambitious for the times. The first name of Bras Basah Road, by the way, was College Street.

While the school buildings gradually extended on either side, the original core remained at the centre. However, Raffles Institution was not known by its present name until 1903, when the school was taken over from the trustees by the Colony Government.

Raffles Girls' School began as the girls' department of the old Singapore Institution in 1844, and did not get its own home on a separate site until 1881.

In that panorama of 19th Century Singapore that one saw between Stamford Road and Bras Basah Road as one rode to town in 1923 it was Raffles Girls' School that exhibited the first modern architecturè, when it got its splendid new building at the end of Victoria Street in 1925. It still was the only Government

English school for girls in Singapore, the Education Department being content to leave the rest of that field to the missions, Roman Catholic and Protestant — chiefly American Methodist, but also Anglican and Presbyterian. But Raffles Girls' School was the premier Girls' school, not only in the eyes of the Education Department but of many old Eurasian families, whose daughters had been educated there for generations.

The next advance in modernisation was when the convent built its new secondary department opposite the Cathedral of the Good Shepherd, on the other side of Victoria Street. Two other leading English schools used this historic strip of land on the other side of the Stamford Road canal. For the boys of St. Joseph's Institution in Bras Basah Road the open space between Bencoolen Street and Queen Street was their sports field, and this was used also by the Anglo-Chinese School, which was then in Coleman Street, at the foot of Fort Canning Hill.

The Y.M.C.A. used to have five grass courts on this land too, but lost then when these developments began in 1924; and I am indebted to Rowland Lyne, who was a resident and observer of Stamford Road for 43 years, for many details lost in my own memories.

For the Singapore of the Centenary the names of all those schools of the past; and some of the thoughts they conjured up for residents who knew something of local history were recorded at that time by a former British headmaster of the Education Department, H. Bazell:

> *"Founded by Raffles himself, the College, now Raffles Institution, is the only scholastic link with the distant past. In its history is contained the story of how the children were neglected until the community, and later the Government, had learnt to appreciate the wider outlook of Raffles.*
>
> *Next must come the history of the various missionary bodies, who, in healthy rivalry first of*

> *all for the good of their pupils, kept aloft the torch of learning, but later, sought in unchristian competition their own advancement.*
>
> *The East India Company gave way to the Colonial authorities, but the time for educational awakening was not yet.*
>
> *Finally, after a hundred years' lethargy, the Government, roused by the more enlightened activity of a foreign mission, has decided to contemplate a college of its own.*
>
> *If then, at last, Raffles's dreams are to be realised in a new Raffles College, the story of the past, with its efforts and its past failures (in the Centenary volumes)... would be a fitting introduction to a more successful future."*

And that indeed is what the future has been, for educationists and the youth of Singapore, ever since. It was, by the way, a proposal by the American Methodist Mission to found a college of higher education that spurred the startled colonial bureaucrats into planning for Raffles College.

In St. Andrew's Road in 1923 was the most remarkable period picture of all: the offices of the Municipality crammed into two very old and very large European residences that had stood there since the first British merchants lived in the centre of the new Settlement, close to their godowns on the other side of the River.

They were two-storeyed, and connected by an outdoor gallery on the upper floor. Together they formed a veritable labyrinth of dark corridors, staircases, creaking wooden floors and wide verandahs, through which I had to find my way once a month when I went there to report the meetings of the Municipal Commissioners.

On Connaught Drive I once saw the last of the Municipal lamp-lighters making his rounds at sunset. He had a long pole which he hooked on to a switch at the top of the iron standard to turn on the gas lamp. I suppose he made a similar round at dawn, but I never saw that. Singapore streets were first lit by gas in 1864. (Before that it had only been the feeble light of oil lamps, probably burning coconut or whale oil). A local company founded in that year supplied the gas until 1900, when the Geylang gasworks were taken over by the Municipality.

The gas lamps on Connaught Drive were already on their way out when I made the mental note recorded above, for street lighting elsewhere in central Singapore was by electricity. This had begun in 1906, but in 1923 the Singapore Municipality was still in the humiliating situation of being dependent for the city's electricity on the Electric Tramway Company, plans to build its own power station having been held up by the war.

In North Bridge Road, standing back in a shady compound, was another of the old European residences, a large two-storeyed house which had found a new use as the hostel for officers of the British merchant marine when they needed accommodation ashore.

When Ager pointed it out to me, on that first day when he was driving me to my boarding house, he remarked, "Conrad used to stay there ....." That was ten years before his time, but when he arrived in 1898 Conrad was still remembered in shipping circles in Singapore, not as the famous author he later became, but as the young second officer on the Arab-owned steamer *Vidal* sailing to the remote little river ports of Dutch East Borneo.

In Coleman Street there was a shabby old hotel, long past the days when it had had a European clientele as the Hotel de la Paix, which also claimed an association with Conrad. It still called itself a hotel when I first noticed it, but was obviously one of the seediest class. Attracted by an indefinable air of distinction, however, I stepped inside and saw at once a faded but unmistakable quality of interior design, and in the spacious lobby paved with the old tiles, that spoke of better days. But it was not until after the World War, when a new and more scholarly generation of local historians began looking into the past, that I learnt the story of the Hotel de la Paix.

It was the house that G.D. Coleman, the first Government architect and public works engineer in the new settlement (duties which he combined with superintendent of convicts) built for himself. Coleman died in 1844, and his tombstone is one of those of the East India Company period preserved on what used to be known as Fort Canning Hill and is now Central Park.

At the other end of the city, in the port area, was another old building with a very different history: the Istana Lama at Telok Blangah, in 1923 a rather disreputable old hotel in a compound off Keppel Road, but once a Malay palace, for that was where the Maharajah of Johore lived with his followers before he moved to his new capital at Johore Bahru in 1880.

He was known as Temenggong Abu Bakar until 1868, when he took the title of Maharaja; and five years after he moved into his new Istana at Johore Bahru he was officially recognised as Sultan. Two ancestors of the present Sultan of Johore, the Temenggong who signed the treaty with Raffles and his son, lie in the graveyard of the old mosque at Telok Blangah.

In 1923, and for some years later, there still was a Malay fishing kampong built out over the water in the mangrove-lined inlet off Keppel Harbour overlooked by the Istana Lama. The kampong and the inlet have long since been obliterated by port development.

23

Life In Cavenagh Road

WHAT WAS LIFE LIKE IN THE BOARDING HOUSE in Cavenagh Road for young and active men without a car, without girl friends, without television or radio entertainment in the evenings?

Well, there certainly were moods and moments when it was just as slow, dull and monotonous as it must seem to readers attuned to the mobility, variety and tempo of life in Singapore today. Our main interests were our jobs and our prospects in the firms we worked for, the games we watched or played at the Singapore Cricket Club (S.C.C.) after office hours or during the weekend, and such social life as the boarding-house district afforded.

But within those narrow limits I think those ghosts of the past would agree with me that our memories of life in Cavenagh Road are better than might be supposed, a few of them so much better in fact that it is a pleasure to recall them. Cavenagh Road was a much pleasanter place to live in than that roaring river of traffic between Orchard Road and Bukit Timah Road can be today.

All things are relative. Most of my fellow boarders had seen service in the 1914 - 18 war on the Western Front or the Middle East, the North Sea or the Atlantic. They thought themselves lucky to be alive. Again, most of them had been living in digs in British cities before they came out. Mrs Matthews' establishment was a lot more sociable, and more spacious, than that. It was certainly a vast improvement on my lonely bedsitter in a workingclass terrace on Balkerne Hill, Colchester.

Once or twice a week we might stop off at the S.C.C. after work, or play tennis somewhere else, but most days we would be back at the boarding house in time for a late afternoon tea, and that was often quite a jolly affair. Mrs Matthews made a special occasion of it, serving sandwiches and cakes on her long table at the end of the dining hall; and as the rickshaws deposited her boarders one by one at the front porch they joined her on the equally long settee and relaxed after the day's work.

After dinner we might go for a walk. Cars were so few and far between in Cavenagh Road in 1923 that we could stroll down the middle of the road without ever giving a thought to traffic. But we were peculiarly fortunate in that we could also walk off the public road, by courtesy of His Excellency the Governor.

As for life without cars, well — you don't miss what you have never had. You took that for granted in the boarding-house district because that was the way it had always been. When old residents of the European business community left for Home on retirement and published their reminiscences in the *Straits Times* or the *Free Press,* we realised that life was going on in our boarding-house, and in dozens like it, almost exactly as it had done when our seniors were juniors themselves in the years between the turn of the century and the 1916 - 18 war.

As for life without girls ..... that was a different matter altogether. The Scotsman of Glasgow in the room next to mine once showed me a letter. It ended: "I love you, Jean." They had been lovers alone in the house for a week while his parents were away. But he was on a five-year agreement. What hope was there that Jean would wait for him, or he for her? Whatever the outcome, he would almost certainly have to wait until he went Home on leave before he had a girl friend again. At the Raffles and the Adelphi there were regular "tea dances" as they were called — around six o'clock, after office hours — and some junior assistants were seen at them; but you could only hope to find a partner if you moved in a more fashionable social set than ours.

Saturday afternoons (after tiffin and a siesta) were usually no problem in the boarding house, since that was when the interclub games or Malaya Cup fixtures were played on the Padang during the football or cricket seasons. Or we played tennis at the S.C.C. or on the Y.M.C.A. courts or elsewhere — for you would find a tennis party in progress on a private court everywhere in the suburbs on a Saturday afternoon in those days.

Sometimes on a Saturday night we would go to "the pictures", as the cinema was called, and that is another jolly memory — three or four lighthearted young men riding down Orchard Road in rickshaws on a moonlight night, heading for the old Alhambra in Beach Road. And there we could hear the junks swaying and creaking with the tide as we watched the screen, for the windows at the back of the dress circle upstairs (where the European patrons always sat) were open to the harbour outside. But the black-and-white silent films, with a single pianist mechanically strumming an accompaniment, were often not worth the effort of getting there.

Incidentally, I do not recollect ever seeing Asiatic patrons in that dress circle, although there was certainly no colour bar at the box office. No doubt it was because Chinese and Indian women of middleclass families would not be willing to accompany their Westernised husbands to such a public place in those days.

On Sunday mornings we went to the Swimming Club at Tanjong Rhu (then, like the S.C.C., a strictly European club). The club put on a launch from Johnston's Pier, for the many younger members who did not have their own transport, and it was a delightful run across the bay. The Swimming Club was a male preserve all day on Sundays (though not on weekdays), with a curry tiffin laid on for those who wanted it, and we swam off the beach in twelve feet of water at high tide. The theory was that sharks would not cross the sandbank beyond, and that held good for half a century or more — until one afternoon in 1926 a shark attacked an Australian girl who was on a visit to Singapore. It took off her leg when she dived into deep water, and she died within ten minutes. After that, a concrete pagar was built.

But it was only on Sunday mornings when there was a high tide that we could go to the Swimming Club. It would not have been worth while at low tide. Those Sundays in the boarding house could be very long, hot and boring, for there was nothing else to do, except perhaps half-hearted tennis on the coarse grass of the court in the afternoon.

The only swimming pool in the city available to us at that time was one run by the Y.M.C.A. on Fort Canning which had formerly been an army reservoir. This was very overcrowded on Sunday mornings, and since the water was not chlorinated, the hygiene will not bear thinking about. However, there were times when it was better than nothing.

During the wet weather of the north-east monsoon, getting enough exercise could be a problem. You never saw anyone jogging on suburban roads, but sometimes in desperation on a rainy afternoon we were reduced to going for a run along the railway track at the bottom of the mangosteen orchard.

An unhappy memory of that first year in Cavenagh Road is of being continually hard-up on $300 a month. After paying Mrs Matthews half of that — and then budgeting for dhoby, room-boy, rickshaw puller, Wing Loong, Robinson and Co. (that tuxedo), club chits and tiffin in town — there was little or no spending money left for the following month; and I sometimes had to draw on the *Straits Times* manager in advance. With his prewar memories, he had not caught up with the postwar cost of living, and I was too timid to tell him so.

Mrs Matthews' establishment was a medium-priced and average one. I could have economised a bit by moving elsewhere, but it seemed simpler to stay put. There were cheaper boarding houses, with charges going down to as low as $100 or less a month — but they were dreadful places, with basic facilities.

There were also more expensive and select establishments, with rates up to $175 or more a month, and in those you might find a young European married couple, as yet unable to afford a bungalow, living in a bedsitter or two rooms. The soul-destroying boredom of a wife in such a situation can be imagined. Mornings with nothing but bridge, mahjong, coffee and gossip (or scandal) .....

There was a huge place called The Mansion — it actually had been a family mansion before it had come down in the world — on the high ground above Tank Road that offered the whole gamut of boarding-house charges; and there were others up bosky backwaters like Mount Elizabeth that were even more pleasantly situated than ours in Cavenagh Road.

* * *

One compensation for the restrictions of rickshaw transport — as seen in retrospect, though hardly appreciated as such at the time — was that in our boarding house we often had to be content with the simple, oldfashioned and almost forgotten pleasure of just going for a walk. The consequence of that was that we explored historically interesting localities and streets on foot, whereas our successors arriving in later years, able to run a car and living farther out, never got to know the inner suburbs at all.

A hundred yards down Cavenagh Road was the side entrance to the Government House Domain: a pair of massive gateposts and an iron gate, never closed. The main entrance was in Orchard Road. This one was disused and deserted, except for the occasional walker like ourselves and the cars of the Colonial Secretary and the Under Secretary, who lived in large bungalows along the private road to which this gate gave access.

Private it was nominally, but the whole Domain — today one of the most strictly guarded areas of Singapore — was open to the public, except for the landscaped gardens around Government House. Anyone could walk through the main gates in Orchard Road unchallenged by the policeman on duty there, and the Cavenagh Road entrance did not even have that token of security.

There was a guardhouse near Government House, manned by

the regiment in garrison, but one never saw either soldiers or policemen when walking in the lower Domain. I suppose if one had strayed off the road on the grassy slopes where young M.C.S. recruits living in the Cadets Bungalow put in some golf practice one might have been ticked off for trespassing, but otherwise there were no restrictions.

I remember with particular pleasure our after-dinner strolls down Cavenagh Road and thence under the avenue of tall tembusu trees to which the Domain gate gave access. During the flowering season the night air was heavy with their fragrance, while innumerable flying foxes rustled and squawked as they sought the nectar in the canopy overhead.

The tembusu, one of the most beautiful of native Malayan trees, (though rare in the north of the Peninsula), was then found all over the Tanglin district; and at the flowering season Tamil coolies were out trapping the giant bats for the pot by some method or other, while more affluent hunters farther out along Ayer Rajah Road and other roads were bringing them down with shotguns. The flying fox has a rank smell as well as a revolting appearance, but its flesh was nevertheless regarded as a poor man's gourmet dish if you knew how to cook it.

Debouching from the tembusu avenue, we could walk down to Orchard Road or we could cross the Domain to a wicket gate for pedestrians on the other side which gave access to Mount Sophia. From there we could go on to a little park and disused reservoir on top of Mount Emily, where there was a panoramic view of the city lights and harbour at night; or we could continue our walk down one of the two very interesting old residential streets that led downhill to Dhoby Ghaut. That was still a distinctly Eurasian and Jewish quarter, with an extraordinary variety of small bungalows perched on steep slopes and approached by flights of steps from the hilly streets.

Another interesting walk from Cavenagh Road was into the very different but almost equally old residential quarter on the other side of Orchard Road, where the compound houses of a wealthier class along streets like Oxley Rise could only be glimpsed behind high stone walls and their private courtyards.

Further up Orchard Road, passing under the railway bridge which crossed that street when the line ended at Tank Road, we could walk up Cairnhill Road and adjacent streets that were another preserve of the Asiatic middle-class, lined with long rows of fine terrace houses, always kept in good order by the Chinese, Indian and other local families whose homes they were.

The "European" reporters who followed me on the *Straits Times* between the wars — recruited in Britain, Australia and New Zealand — had a better life in many ways; but none of them ever saw those places or had those memories.

24

The Unknown Highway

ONE SUNDAY AFTERNOON in our boarding house, when the tennis court was wet after rain and there was nothing else to do, four of us decided to go for a country drive. None of us had a car — in fact, there was only one car among the dozen bachelors in the boarding house, and that a battered old jalopy shared by two older men — so the only way we could have this outing was by hiring a car from a garage.

This was a not uncommon form of recreation, especially for romantic reasons, at the higher salary levels of the boarding-house district; but it was a luxury we young men could very rarely afford, for it cost three dollars an hour, with a Malay syce supplied (and he, by the way, did not get or expect a tip for our three-hour excursion). But we were bored and needed a change.

We took the Woodlands road, as it was then called, so that was my first drive across the island. The Woodlands road was in no sense the highway leading to the North that it became a few years later. It was still a country road surfaced with laterite, so narrow beyond Bukit Timah that two vehicles could hardly pass, and serving two or three small villages along the way.

We were already out in a rural landscape at Bukit Timah, then a rather large village of shophouses dependent for trade on the workers at two Chinese-owned rubber factories processing the native rubber imported from Sumatra and elsewhere.

On the steep rise in the road beyond the village (the cutting through the ridge had not yet been made) there was beautiful virgin jungle on both sides of the road; and, beyond that, mainly rubber estates, but also small holdings here and there where Chinese squatters were growing cash crops of fruit and vegetables for the City markets, while living on their own produce, pigs and poultry.

Several miles from the Straits the road turned aside at the then impassable Marsling mangrove swamps, and followed a roundabout route over hilly country to Woodlands. It still exists as a side-road to industrial estates off the motorway today.

At Woodlands the road ended at a bluff overlooking the little railway station and the jetty for the F.M.S. Railways passenger ferry to Johore Bahru — and I still remember that moment when we gazed across the mile-wide Straits and at the great granite bank of the Causeway just emerging from the surface of the water.

Driving back that evening in our open-tourer car, I remember how rare it was to meet another vehicle on that country road, and how remote that dark and silent countryside seemed from the suburbs to which we were returning. For all the signs of life there were, we might have been in the unknown country on the other side of the Johore Straits, instead of only ten miles from Singapore.

My memories of the Woodlands road go back beyond my own time, passed on to me by that *Straits Times* oldtimer, Ager, and now passed on by me. In his early days he once travelled the whole way from the city to Woodlands by rickshaw, 14 miles across the island, with only one change, at Bukit Timah village; and he came back the same way.

The purpose of that Sunday outing was to spend a day at the Johore Bahru gambling farm, and it must have been before 1905, when the Singapore-Kranji railway was opened — and carried half a million passengers in its first year, so great was the novelty. The railway was built by a private company, but was taken over by the F.M.S. Railways when the main line from Kuala Lumpur reached Johore Bahru in 1909.

My memories of the Woodlands road also preserve a story I heard from an elderly Eurasian resident many years later. As a small boy he was taken by his father on the horse-coach that ran from a hotel in Coleman Street to the Woodlands ferry — the objective again being the gambling farm on the other side of the Johore Straits. That was a favourite Sunday diversion of Singapore people until the Sultan closed down the gambling farm, and its premises became the Johore Bahru resthouse (and survived as such until after the World War.)

Another oldtimer of the European community in my young days, E.A. Brown, cycled over the Woodlands road in 1901 with a friend to spend the weekend in Johore Bahru, and in his book *Indiscreet Memories* he recalls that after Bukit Panjang — which he describes as "a native village in a small clearing" — the narrow laterite road entered magnificent virgin jungle.

Here they passed a small road-roller left derelict beside the road, and the explanation was that a tiger had sprung out of the jungle, killed the driver and carried off the bullock drawing the roller. The road then ended at Kranji, and here they took a sampan across the Straits.

On the way back, because of tyre trouble, Brown had to put his bicycle in a rickshaw at Bukit Panjang, and himself in another. They did the journey of eleven miles back to his boarding house, he says, "including the climb up the hill at Bukit Timah, in five minutes under the hour, without changing rickshaws or pullers."

The pullers were running in the cool of the evening (having left the village at 6.20 p.m.), but even so, that was surely a feat of endurance and fitness that would be regarded with respect in the marathon running clubs of today.

* * *

Early in 1924 — some months before the completion of the road across the Johore Causeway — the manager of Borneo Motors, Webster by name, invited the editor of the *Straits Times* to send a

THE UNKNOWN HIGHWAY 141

reporter to join a pioneer car journey he was going to make from Singapore to Kuala Lumpur.

In thus seeking publicity I do not think that that business manager foresaw the enormous increase in road travel from Singapore that was to come in the next few years. No doubt that was because Webster could not foresee the enormous influx of new cars that was to come either. Borneo Motors' new showrooms in Orchard Road only had one new model in the window, and that for demonstration purposes. All the motor firms in Orchard Road were importing no more than a trickle of new cars, for the factories overseas were still gearing up for peacetime production after the 1914 - 18 war and subsequent slump.

No, what Webster wanted to do was to show Singapore motorists how easy it was to do something they never did at that time — transport their cars across the Johore Straits and explore the hinterland beyond. At that time most Singapore motorists did not even know that that was possible, or what the roads would be like on the other side. Unless they visited friends on Johore rubber estates they would not even know whether it was possible to get through to Batu Pahat from Johore Bahru by road — although the trunk road through the Peninsula had been completed before the Great War.

In the first decade of the century there had been one of two adventurous European motorists in Singapore who had taken their cars into Selangor and Pahang (by sea to Port Swettenham). There was even a tourist agency in Kuala Lumpur that advertised a road trip to Singapore before the 1914 - 18 war — though that actually ended by putting the car on a coasting steamer at Muar. However, all such adventures had been forgotten by a younger generation in Singapore after the war.

The car which Webster used was a long-forgotten American make called the Good Maxwell — so called because the first Maxwell had not been a success — for which Borneo Motors were the agents; and he took along a relief driver, a European colleague from his own firm. To save time, he sent on the relief driver with the car the previous day, and had it transported across the Straits on the pontoon ferry operated by the F.M.S. Railways; so it was waiting for us on the other side. Webster and I left Singapore at before dawn in another car, and crossed the Straits in the passenger ferry launch.

Incidentally, the pontoon ferry was a very busy one. It transported 58,000 railway wagons across the Straits in the peak year of 1921. But the F.M.S. Railways would take a car if you asked them — which apparently no car owner on either side of Johore Straits ever did at that time.

Well, everything went according to plan. The Good Maxwell ran perfectly, and we made unexpectedly good time, with two expert drivers pushing the car fast but carefully on the narrow twisting laterite roads that then made up most of the links in the trunk road from Johore Bahru to the north. In the hilly rubber country of South Johore, in particular, I recall many bends and blind corners that have long since been straightened out.

At the Ayer Hitam road junction the present direct route north through Negri Sembilan had not yet been constructed, and we had to turn towards the coast and cross the river ferries at Batu Pahat and Muar. Even with those interesting but time-wasting interruptions, we arrived at the Station Hotel, Kuala Lumpur, comfortably in time for afternoon tea.

I went back to Singapore the same night by the mail train, and wrote about our trip as if we had been travelling through country that was completely strange and unknown to our Singapore readers, as indeed it was. They were surprised to learn that it could be done, and done so easily. Nevertheless, I do not think that my glowing report inspired any of them to follow suit, for unless you could spare a long weekend or a longer holiday it was simply not worth while to put your car on the pontoon ferry.

Borneo Motors' publicity stunt may have paid dividends later on, however, in that it opened the eyes of Singapore motorists to the road system that already existed in southern Malaya; and they took advantage of it as soon as they could.

The River Route

SEVERAL MONTHS AFTER I JOINED THE *STRAITS TIMES* my eccentric but very good planter friend Calder — whom we have met earlier in these recollections — turned up at the office one day and invited me to go back with him for a weekend at Kota Tinggi. Our journey there is worth recalling, for it was soon to become a thing of the past. Travel to Kota Tinggi was still by the old river route — old indeed, for it had been used since that was the High Fort of a Malay sultan of Johore in the 16th Century, and probably farther back than that.

Our journey began at the Hylam Kongsi, which was the name for the waterfront area on the other side of Beach Road opposite Raffles Hotel. At that time there were no modern buildings between Raffles Hotel and its harbour view, and the water was only a hundred yards or so from Beach Road. Here, at a landing place of some sort, we took a sampan and were rowed out to a little steamer anchored in the bay.

This part of the harbour was the anchorage for local sailing craft, Chinese junks, boats of several Indonesian rigs, and Indian tongkangs; and the many masts and differently shaped hulls presented a picturesque contrast with the "mosquito fleet" of coastal and inter-island steamers farther along the waterfront. However, the steamboats trading up the Johore River were much smaller, and anchored among the sailing craft. Ours was hardly more than a glorified launch, though it must have had a hundred or more deck passengers, mostly Chinese.

Calder was accompanied by a young M.C.S. officer named Bryson, stationed at Kota Tinggi, and they had been spending the weekend with two Malay girls in a seaside kampong at Changi. I envied them that experience; but it could not have been mine in any case without the fluent conversational Malay and the familiarity with kampong folk that those two possessed.

After coasting along Singapore Island and turning into the Johore River the channel gradually narrowed until we were twisting and turning between muddy mangrove-lined banks, with rubber and jungle on the higher ground behind. What I thought was a dead tree trunk on the mud suddenly slithered into the water as we passed — a huge crocodile. It was very hot in the small open enclosure reserved for first-class passengers, but a most interesting run up the river. There were stops at several kampong jetties on the way up, and we reached Kota Tinggi in about four hours.

That was how the people of Kota Tinggi and down-river travelled to and from Singapore before the Johore Causeway was constructed. The river steamer transported not only passengers but rubber and other produce to the city, and brought back supplies for the shopkeepers of that outstation.

It would have been possible, after cars came in, for the small white community of Kota Tinggi — planters and officials and their wives — to drive to Johore Bahru, cross the Straits by ferry, and catch the train to Singapore, but it was more direct and convenient to go by the river route. A European estate manager in the Kota Tinggi district was the local agent for the Chinese shipowners in Singapore, and the recipient of much legpulling in the club over the service and amenities (or lack of them) provided. The only toilet facility on the little steamer was an iron cage over the stern, used by both sexes.

At Kota Tinggi I stayed in the resthouse for Government officers on the padang, where Calder and Bryson were living. In the late afternoon they took out a Rugby football to kick around, and they had the padang to themselves. The silence and remoteness of the place made an instant impression upon me. It seemed like a different country from Singapore, as indeed it was.

Bryson was stationed in Kota Tinggi to supervise the rubber restriction scheme in the smallholdings (Malay and Chinese) along the river, and he was provided with a motorboat for that purpose, but the engine would not start. When it was eventually taken to pieces they found that someone had thrown a spanner in the works. The young M.C.S. officer was not wanted in the native rubber plantations along the river, nor did the owners want the production quotas and ban on new planting that it was his duty to enforce.

As I had to be back in time to start work on Monday morning I left on Sunday by hire-car for Johore Bahru, where I walked across the railway track on the unfinished Causeway, and took another hire-car on the other side to Singapore.

It was dark by that time, and a marvellous memory of that drive through the hilly rubber estates beyond Woodlands is of the myriads of fireflies in the bushes on either side of the laterite road, switching on and off their jewelled lights in mysterious and perfect synchronisation. In later years fireflies became more and more rare on Singapore Island, and I suppose many people living there now have never seen a firefly at all.

26
Inside The Colour Bar

ANOTHER PERSONAL SIDELIGHT ON THE PERIOD — and a confession I would rather not make — must seem to anyone living in Singapore today the most extraordinary of all — the fact that I was now living entirely within a tiny minority of the population, with no social intercourse whatever on the other side of the invisible but real barriers surrounding the European community, and that as a newcomer from England I seem to have accepted the transition into this exclusive way of life without surprise or even questioning.

Well, of course it was not extraordinary then. Not only the Europeans but all the other communities lived in separate racial compartments, and the womenfolk in Chinese, Indian and Malay families were even more conservative than their white sisters (if that nice verbal touch is appropriate in the context of the times, which I doubt).

Moreover, for the five thousand men, women and children of the European community the Asiatic population of nearly half a million seemed an alien and impenetrable world. In Chinatown, the Indian quarter along Serangoon Road, and the Malay and Arab quarter around the Sultan Mosque, all races still wore their own costumes and spoke their own languages. So did the Chinese and Indian merchants and dealers I used to see transacting business with European firms in Raffles Place and thereabouts.

But that is not the whole truth, for there were English-speaking communities out there too, in particular the Eurasian community; and in my daily life and work there were human contacts outside my own community which I could have followed up if I had not been indoctrinated from the first to think of myself as a member of the ruling race and to behave accordingly. Let me give three illustrations.

When I sat at the Press table in the Supreme Court the *Free Press* reporter beside me was often a young Eurasian named Jerry Hogan (though I never knew his first name was Jerry until long after he died as a member of the Singapore Volunteer Corps on the Death Railway in Siam). He was a credit to Raffles Institution where he had been educated, presentable in every way, a competent reporter, and a much better shorthand writer than I was. Yet it never occurred to me, after we left the court, to invite him to have a drink with me at the Cricket Club across the way — never, because I could not have taken him in there. I do not know whether he could have taken me into his own club at the other end of the Padang, but self-respect would have forbidden any such onesided overture. We could at least have had a friendly cup of coffee in High Street, but I never thought of that either.

In my boarding house there was a shy young fellow, a Eurasian of about the same age as most of us, who slipped in and out of the house like a ghost, hardly exchanging a word with the European boarders. He was Mrs Matthews' only son; and if we could put the clock back, with the racial and social freedom of today, we would invite him to sit down with us and have a drink or two; we would know what his job was, and something about his interests outside the boarding house. But it never happened. No such gesture of friendliness was ever made. And all we knew about him was that he was a worry to his mother, having drifted from one job to another (which might explain why the poor lady had a drink problem).

Soon after I arrived I was sent to Johore Bahru to report the annual meeting of the Johore Planters' Association. I was fresh from Home, with no racial prejudices whatsoever, keen to learn and interested in everything and everybody. Sitting in the room where the meeting was to be held was another reporter, an Asiatic of dark complexion — and to my surprise he was reading the Times Literary Supplement. This instantly proved a common bond, and we had an animated conversation and tiffin together in the Johore resthouse afterwards. That was Francis Cooray, a Sinhalese from Colombo. Some months later I was sent to Kuala Lumpur to report a meeting of the Federal Council, and I met Cooray again at the Press table. But this time I instantly sensed a change. Cooray was reserved, withdrawn, no longer friendly. That was because I had unconsciously changed too. The unspoilt young Englishman had become the new colonial. The insidious evil of white superiority had entered into his soul.

I cherish all the more, therefore, a memory of the young Indian reporter on the *Malaya Tribune* named Davies whom I used to meet in the police courts. He belonged to a local-born Indian family, and his mother was a feminist and a nationalist in her contacts with European women half a century before her time. One day Davies invited me to his home for a Sunday curry tiffin. By that time I had a motor cycle, so I rode out to his house, which was a small bungalow in a large compound of coconut palms and flowering shrubs at Upper Serangoon. So cheap was the cost of living then that Davies could afford all that on his reporter's pay. Anyhow, we had a very nice Indian curry, served by his shy and pretty little wife, who, however did not sit down with us or talk to me at all. She was Indian too, and wore the sari. That is a good memory, but it never happened again. And where Jerry Hogan's home was, and what his family life was like, I never knew.

When I pause to reflect that a Eurasian resident in his fifties could have claimed in 1923 that he had been born in the year when the Straits Settlements became a Crown colony, I realise the local traditions that I might have heard in Eurasian families at that time, and which I never knew anything about.

Older residents in their sixties would have been born in

Singapore when it was still a possession of the East India Company; and their memories of childhood would have been during the nine years in which the Settlement remained under the Government of Bengal after the British Government abolished John Company.

For example, the Leicester family ..... it is only since I wrote my memories of Cavenagh Road that I discovered what that name must have recalled to Henry Barnaby Leicester, who was an old man when I was a young one.

> *"I have a pretty vivid recollection in the 'sixties of Colonel (afterwards Major-General) Orfeur Cavenagh, the last of our Governors under the Indian regime. He had lost a leg during the Indian Mutiny, but, although encumbered with a wooden substitute, was always on horseback, from which he used to review the Indian troops on the old Esplanade.*
>
> *The infantry, composed of Madras sepoys, were clad in scarlet tunics and white trousers. Their headgear consisted of a red, round, close-fitting cap without a peak, with a broad band falling behind and overlapping the nape of the neck. The artillery, also Indian, wore white tunics and black trousers, with tall black, shiny hats, something after the style of the Parsee hat.*

However, if we leave these rather wistful musings, and go back to the realities of everyday living in the Cavenagh Road boarding house, there would have been precious little chance of talking to old Mr Leicester anyway. Better late than never ..... it has been a pleasure to meet him at last in the memories he recorded for *One Hundred Years of Singapore*.

Finally I want to relate the salutary shock that I received as a member of the European (i.e. British) community when I visited my American Methodist missionary friends. The Rev. F.H.

Sullivan had met the *Glaucus* when I arrived, but had quickly noted the look of perplexity — and, I am ashamed to add, perhaps consternation — when he told me that he had come to welcome me to Methodist fellowship in Singapore or something of the sort. That was the last thing I was expecting at that moment.

Unknown to me, the Rev. G.T. Peet had written from his Wesleyan Methodist manse at St. Mawes, Cornwall, to the minister of Wesley Church. My father had been a missionary in India himself in his younger years, and I suppose he wanted to safeguard his son against the perils of life in the East, particularly bachelor loneliness. Anyway, this friendly American minister did not take umbrage at my apparently ungrateful response, but left me with the *Straits Times* manager, promising to get in touch when I had settled down; and he kept that promise.

So one Sunday evening I was invited to dinner with the Sullivan family, and while I was there one of the Chinese ministers of the Methodist Mission arrived to talk about some personal trouble. I was instantly struck by the warm friendliness and kindness with which the Rev. Goh Hood Keng was received in this American missionary home, by the atmosphere of genuine and unforced racial equality. I had been in a number of European bungalows by then, but I had never seen an Asiatic guest in them.

* * *

In the white community we invariably referred to the yellow, black and brown population among which we lived as "the Asiatics". The present-day term "Asian" did not come into use until after the World War, and in fact I first became aware of it when I resumed work on the resuscitated *Straits Times* after the internment. There was never any official directive on this change.

I can only guess that in Anglo-American radio propaganda during the war they felt that "Asiatic" smacked too much of the prewar era for their listeners in the enemy-occupied countries.

Or perhaps it was just that during the war years, for the first time, the whole region became known to the news media as South-East Asia. Anyway, Asiatics they were for us then, and nobody in the Chinese, Indian, or Malaysian communities ever thought of questioning it.

By the time I arrived, however, there had been an even earlier shift of verbal etiquette, as it were, for before the Great War the European residents of Singapore referred to everybody else (except the Eurasians) as "the natives".

One sees this in the pre-1914 files of the *Straits Times,* in many European reminiscences of the period, and all through the Centenary volumes, *One Hundred Years of Singapore* (published in 1921), in articles contributed by some of the most senior European residents, official and unofficial, still living there.

As late as 1932 "the natives" appear again, in E.A. Brown's locally published memoirs, but as that oldtimer had come out from England in 1901 he could be excused for using the term that still came naturally to him. No doubt it went back to the early days of the Settlement, when most of the Europeans came from India, where it was in general use.

I myself cannot remember any senior man of the European community of my junior years ever speaking of the Asiatics as "the natives"; but I certainly did hear a few white women doing so, and it grated upon my ears even then, as seemingly imbued with the instinctive colour prejudice that was so much stronger in their sex than in their menfolk — though in reality I suppose it often meant no more than a vague reference to the alien and unknown environment outside their sheltered homes and their husbands' clubs and offices.

Anyway "the natives" would certainly have had an offensive ring about it in print in the *Straits Times* or anywhere else in public discussion between the wars. It was one of those curious, silent shifts that take place almost unconsciously in social history.

How odd it seems in retrospect that we always referred to ourselves as "the European community" when nearly all of us were certainly not Europeans in the Continental sense! Indeed, even now, when Britain is a member of the European Economic Community, my compatriots at Home still regard the nations on the other side of the English Channel as foreigners.

There were a few hundred true Europeans in Singapore between the wars: the Dutch, the Swiss, the French, who formed separate little communities, with their own social life, their own clubs, and, for the Dutch, their own school (which is still there in Orange Grove Road to this day). Before the Great War the important and wealthy German community had had the finest club of all, the Teutonia, afterwards the Goodwood Park Hotel; and in the decade before the World War the German business and shipping men came back again. The Americans were another separate white community, mostly in the rubber trade and shipping. But they were not numerous enough to have their own school until after World War Two.

When I and my contemporaries spoke of "the European community" what we nearly always meant was our own colonial society: the British business and professional people one saw around Raffles Place, the civil servants and other Government officers in Empress Place, the engineers and other British employees of the Municipality and the Harbour Board, and of course their wives and families.

The "British" label was only used in newspaper comment or other public discussion when it was necessary to specify British interests, commercial or colonial, in any issue of local politics. In any other context, particularly the social one, we were "Europeans". That is what the Asiatic and the Eurasian communities called us; and that is how we spoke of ourselves, whether we came from London or Manchester or anywhere else in the distant country that we thought of as Home.

This seems more odd than ever when one recalls the European Association of Singapore. This conservative body, modelled on similar associations in India, was formed between the wars; yet, in spite of its title, it was openly and exclusively an organ of British unofficial opinion. (After the World War it surfaced again, as the British European Association of Singapore, but that title made more sense in the vastly different European and American business and banking community that developed there after independence).

Perhaps the unspoken or even consciously recognised reason for not calling ourselves "the British community" between the wars, when that was almost always what we meant, was that the Eurasians would have claimed to belong to it too — and rightly so, for they were more patriotically and unreservedly British than ourselves.

27
Tuans And Mems

I SUPPOSE THAT if I have any readers in the Asia of today, what they will dislike most is to find me talking about coolies, since that word, above all others, seems to have had distasteful colonial connotations since the World War. In Singapore today this word is heard only as an occasional term of contempt for coarse or rude behaviour in Chinese society.

But when I arrived, and throughout the period between the wars, the whole class of unskilled manual workers in urban and rural Singapore were always referred to as coolies. Only in the Singapore Municipality, and in the printed annual reports of the Straits Settlements Public Works Department, were their daily-paid Indian workers officially designated as labourers.

It was the same upcountry, where European planters and Chinese tin miners invariably referred to their labour forces — whether Indian or Chinese — as coolies; though there again in the Labour Department of the F.M.S. Government they were officially labourers. Everywhere else, and for everybody else, a labourer was a coolie.

Workers of this class were all immigrants from South India or South China. The Chinese coolies were totally illiterate, and nearly all were unmarried, and could never hope to be anything else. The children of the Tamil labour forces on European rubber estates did get a little education, in the estate schools required by the F.M.S. Labour Department (and demanded by the Government of India, as guardian of its people overseas); and marriage was possible for their parents too, since they were provided with a room in the coolie lines (another term still in everyday use) and could live on their joint wages.

There is no denying that both for the European community and the local English-speaking public, in the F.M.S. as in Singapore, a coolie meant not only a labourer but a person at the very bottom of the social and economic scale; but other than that, I do not think it had the offensive connotation that it would have today. The coolie class was simply one of the facts of life. The word appeared in the *Straits Times* almost every day, in one context or another, and the Indian community never took exception to it, as they did to "Klings".

Another local usage that seems odd today was the way we talked of "boys" when we meant a Chinese house-boy or a waiter. In the larger European households there might be two house servants besides the cook and the mistress's personal amah. At a dinner party one might hear the hostess talking about her "No. 1 boy" or her "Kechil Boy" (i.e. the No. 2, a younger one on a smaller wage).

European women usually tried to reach some sort of decent human relationship with their servants, especially those of long standing: and this included addressing them by their first name (or as near as a European could get to it) the exception being the Chinese cook, who was always known by the rather pleasant diminutive of Cookie. In the European boarding houses and bachelor messes and clubs, however, it was always just "Boy"

In the European hotels, if you wanted a drink, you also shouted "Boy", although the Chinese staff (of the same Hylam community as the house servants) were actually impeccably trained and dressed waiters. It was only after the World War that guests were expected to address them as such.

Likewise the waiters in other down-town European haunts, the large cafe-restaurants on the top floor of John Little's and Robinson's department stores and the G.H. Cafe in Battery

Road, were always "boys". They all wore the same sort of dress at work: a white coat with high collar and loose white trousers — and in the hotels the trousers were tied at the ankles and worn with black slippers.

* * *

In the European community of that time the men (down to the latest and most junior assistant) were always addressed as Tuan and the women as Mem, not only when they were at home but everywhere else when they were not speaking to someone in the English-educated class of the Asiatic population.

It has never been explained why a Malay form of address should have become customary for a European man, and an Indian one for his wife. "Mem" was of course an abbreviation of *Memsahib*, and must have been imported from India, but the Anglo-Indian term was never used in full in the Straits Settlements.

Tuan is defined by Winstedt as a term applied "to Malays — both men and women — who do not have higher titles, to a haji of either sex (one who has made the pilgrimage to Mecca), to descendants of the Prophet, or by a lover to his mistress or vice versa". Less romantically, Winstedt adds that Tuan could have the meaning of master (in the sense of employer); and that was what it meant in European homes. As such, no doubt, it was a term of respect. But in town, as used by a Chinese dealer doing business with a European firm, or by the "boys" in the hotels and elsewhere, I do not think that Tuan was anything more than the only possible form of address for people who did not speak English; and the same with Mem for a white woman. (A point to be noted by the anti-colonial satirists of today.)

It was a European community in which Malay was an indispensable means of communication. The Mem would have to speak Malay to Cookie and her other house servants, to the gardener (always called by the Malay word *Kebun*, though he might be a Tamil), to the car driver (always a Malay), to stallholders in the market, and to Chinese shopkeepers. (The Indian dressmakers, jewellers and provision merchants in High Street, then the main shopping street outside Raffles Place, were a more Westernised type and spoke English.) The Tuan during his day down-town would also need Malay to speak to the *tambies* in his office, to the Sikh taxi drivers and the Chinese rickshaw pullers (though the latter only knew three or four words), and to the boys in hotels and clubs and restaurants.

If one was being polite one might call it "bazaar Malay", and that in fact was the *lingua franca* of business in Raffles Place and Chinatown. But Malayan Civil Service officers who had lived in Malay districts upcountry and had learnt the language properly would downgrade much of the Malay they heard in the European community of Singapore still further, and call it pidgin Malay.

In the F.M.S. the M.C.S. were equally critical of what they heard in the European ranks of the Government service outside their own. They spoke scathingly of "P.W.D. Malay". However, they would have agreed that many of the British police officers, foresters and surveyors — Government officers who spent a great deal of time in rural Malaya and among the kampong folk — spoke good colloquial Malay.

The older European residents, both men and women, who had lived in Singapore before the 1914 - 18 war, usually spoke bazaar Malay fluently. Those who had arrived since the war rarely did so, unless they had to acquire it in day-to-day business chaffering — and for most of them the office day did not include that. Theirs was the pidgin Malay.

Even so, everyday speech in the European community, even when talking among themselves, was sprinkled with Malay words to a remarkable extent. They said *makan* when they meant a meal; and if the hostess served dishes of assorted appetisers at a cocktail party (always offered to dinner guests as well) these were *makan kechil*. If they went for an evening drive in the car it was *makan angin* (a delightful Malay expression meaning literally "eat the air").

Several words in the Singapore vocabulary of the 1920s went

back to the Portuguese period in Malacca (1511 - 1641). A wardrobe in a bedroom was always an *almeirah*; the word for fork was *garfu*, and for butter it was *mantega*. These were all Portuguese words that had to be used with the house servants. (But bread was the Indian word *roti*.)

It is curious, by the way, that the Dutch period in Malacca, though even longer, ending in 1795 during the Napoleonic Wars, left behind no words whatever in everyday speech in the Straits Settlements.)

In this chapter, and throughout these recollections, I have used the Romanised Malay phonetic spelling of the period. The new phonemic spelling — whatever that means — adopted in Malaysia for the sake of uniformity with Indonesia would look anachronistic in this context; and in any case I would be quite incapable of transcribing from one to the other, having been mystified by the new spelling of what were once familiar words when I revisited Peninsular Malaysia in the 1970s.

* * *

Much more interesting than bazaar Malay in this local European vocabulary of the 1920s were the Indian words in it that had been used by white residents of Singapore (and in the Eurasian community too) ever since East India Company days. The regime of John Company — its nickname when it ruled India — ended officially in the Straits Settlements in 1867, but in practice the connection with the Bengal Presidency went on for some years longer; and it had left a lasting Anglo-Indian imprint upon the Singapore scene.

Lunch in the European community was invariably tiffin, at home as well as down-town. A house was a bungalow, no matter how big it was, or whether it had more than one storey. Even the huge old rambling official residence of the Colonial Secretary in the Government House Domain was the Colonial Secretary's Bungalow.

The Anglo-Indian word *compound*, for the ground around a

bungalow, was more often used than garden. The *punkah* had been in general use only a few years back. The car driver was the *syce*, a word which went back to the days when the officials and merchants from India kept their horse-carriages in Singapore. The local equivalent of a cab was a gharry. A clerk in a firm in Raffles Place was a krani; the lowly office worker employed to run messages was a *tamby*; and a *serang* in the harbour was a boatswain or launch captain. When European ladies went to their Indian dressmaker (male) in High Street, they spoke of him as their *durzi*.

In Empress Place, however, the *tambies* in the Government offices were known as *peons,* a word which the British had taken over from the Portuguese in India; and the *peons* of the Colonial Secretariat still wore the picturesque and colourful East India Company uniform; a peculiar wide-brimmed hat with a flat crown and a bright red cummerbund, and a white jacket with a similar red sash.

Dhoby Ghaut, the only Indian place-name in the city, was another echo of the same period; and so was Sepoy Lines. Dhoby Ghaut, the open space at the junction of Bras Basah Road and Selegie Road, was where the Indian washermen used to work in the freshwater stream that then ran beside Orchard Road to the sea; and Sepoy Lines, an inner-city area near the General Hospital, was where the East India Company's native troops — withdrawn after the Transfer to the Colonial Office — had had their barracks. And of course Havelock Road and Outram Road were echoes of the Indian Mutiny of 1857.

To my mind, the most interesting and puzzling local word of all that had come down from those days (and one still current in Singapore today) was *godown*, the word used by the business community for the two-storey buildings of the 1860s on the Collyer Quay waterfront, for the old warehouses along the Singapore River, and for the modern cargo sheds on the wharves of the Singapore Harbour Board.

What is the derivation of *godown*, and where does it come from? The Oxford Dictionary says: "probably an adaptation of the

Malay word '*godung*' meaning storehouse." With fear and trembling, I question that august authority, for a retired Calcutta merchant living in my street in South Perth assures me that the word godown is used in the same sense all over India, and has been ever since East India Company times there.

Why should European merchants in India be using a Malay word? And how could it have crossed the Bay of Bengal from the Malay Peninsula in the 17th Century? It would seem more likely that the reverse happened, and that the Malays got this word from the Indian traders who first reached their shores two thousand years ago. A former colleague of mine still resident in Singapore to whom I put this query has been pursuing it on his bookshelves, and has surely come up with the derivation that the O.E.D. missed. R.J. Wilkinson, the Anglo-Malayan scholar, derives the Malay *godung* from the Telegu *gidangi* and/or a similar word in Tamil, both meaning a place where goods are kept. So the word *godown* in present-day Singapore is the most ancient Indian imprint of all.

28
Down The Line

OCCASIONALLY ON A SATURDAY NIGHT, when the monotony of life in Cavenagh Road got too much for the boarders, and too many stengahs had been imbibed, a group of them would set off hilariously on the sort of excursion that was known as "going down the line" (a corruption of "down the line" in Calcutta and Madras): in other words, the brothel quarter.

Singapore's notorious Malay Street, known to seamen and travellers the world over, was only a legend by that time, the French and other white prostitutes having been deported — for racial rather than moral reasons — after the Great War broke out. Malay Street (in the locality at the back of Beach Road) was still there, but was now only a Chinatown lane. The brothels in 1923 (at least those catering for Europeans) were farther out on the semi-rural fringe of the city, along MacPherson Road and Balestier Road, where driveways led into darkened compounds with dim red lamps at the other end.

Actually, "going down the line" often meant no more than a tour of those squalid establishments, the roistering climax of a Saturday-night bachelor beat-up, rather than a longer stay as paying patrons of the Malay and Chinese prostitutes — but that is not to say that it never happened.

On those occasions, as the only teetotaller in the boarding house (now a matter of senile regret), and the son and grandson of Wesleyan ministers, I was the odd man out — I was quite amicably left behind The three care-free Cable Company boys among us had no such inhibitions, and they were much more normal and happier beings for their age than I was during those solitary Saturday nights in Cavenagh Road. I mention this only as a warning that the viewpoint in these recollections is not always an average one.

The Eastern Extension Telegraph Company brought their staff out from Home at eighteen — too young to be launched on life in the East, even though they spent the first two years under idyllic conditions in the Cocos Islands. Perhaps the strict Clunies-Ross and company ban on visiting the kampong on the other side of the lagoon partly explained the fun they had when they kicked over the traces on Saturday nights in Singapore. But the boarders also went "down the line" because there were times when any feminine company was better than none. For it almost literally was none elsewhere. The only times when the average European mercantile assistant could expect to be in the company of a woman of his own race were when he was invited to dinner by married colleagues or friends.

There were said to be only six marriageable girls in the European community when I joined it in 1923. Companionship and friendship, not to say love, such as would have been normal with girls of their own age at home, was out of the question for the junior assistant on his first tour.

There was no equivalent in Singapore to the annual sexual phenomenon of the "Fishing Fleet" in Calcutta; but eligible girls who came out to stay with their parents (after an expensive education in private schools) naturally had marriage in view, and that was only practicable with older men. Soon after I arrived, motherly Mrs Ager was at pains to puncture any romantic illusions I might have been harbouring. "Of course, you won't be able to marry during your first agreement," she said, "because you can't possibly afford to keep a wife and provide a bungalow and servants and all the rest of it on your salary. Perhaps towards the end of your second agreement....." That was five or six years away — but after all, I was only twenty-one.

Actually, I was more fortunate than most of my contemporaries in being on a three-year agreement. Four-year and five-year tours were quite common — more often the latter, in import and export firms. In the Hong Kong Bank and Mercantile Bank it was six years; and in the Chartered Bank it was actually seven years. Moreover, the British banks forbade marriage during the first tour even if the assistant had private means.

To what extent "going down the line" meant more than alcoholic fun and feminity (of a sort) is another matter. There were no novelists, still less sociologists or psychiatrists, to probe the dark side of private and personal life in those days. Only the European doctors practising in Raffles Place and Battery Road could have thrown some light upon it. Only they too knew to what extent the high risk of venereal disease was ever taken or escaped.

The brothels were tolerated, but not officially recognised, still less medically inspected. The police had enough to do with trying to suppress gambling in Chinatown without taking on prostitution as well, in a city in which the sex ratio was still heavily unbalanced in a mainly immigrant coolie class. Moreover Singapore was a great port, and transient customers for the European brothels may well have outnumbered the locals.

There was both a physical and an emotional price to be paid for celibacy during those years of life. Dr Boland, whose rooms were above an English chemist's shop in Raffles Place, told me he repeatedly had patients who were frequently in his surgery as bachelors, but whom he never saw again after they married. He also told me of two older European men sharing a bungalow at which two rickshaws, each bringing a Malay woman, drew up on a routine engagement once a week. It is a pity that no doctor of that period ever wrote his memoirs (particularly the oldest of them all, Sir David Galloway, who had been practising in Raffles Place since before the turn of the century, and was the personal physician to the Sultan of Johore).

When the boarders in Cavenagh Road met for a sociable drink

in the evenings the talk inevitably gravitated towards the same topic — women, but women only in the past, in memory, in their lives before they came out to Singapore. In twelve months of sexual reminiscence (much of it undeniably interesting), I recall only three flesh-and-blood stories of the real thing in our midst.

One Saturday afternoon the Manchester piecegoods man — whose room was near the back stairs — was leaning over his verandah when he caught the eye of Mrs Matthews' Malay ayah in the courtyard below. He signalled; she responded; and a mutually satisfactory meeting in his room followed. But the ayah had been slipping up the back stairs, and when gossip about that reached Mrs Matthews from the servants' quarters she was promptly sent packing. No more romance from that quarter.

Once there was general interest when a white woman came to dwell among us. She was a planter's wife from Johore, on a brief holiday in the city. She obviously hated her life in an estate bungalow, and her hard-drinking and coarse husband as well, as we saw when he arrived to join her. In the meantime, one of the more sophisticated of our group had taken his place.

Most memorable of all was the dream that came true for the young man from Glasgow in the room next to mine. As an employee of a printing firm, he dealt with an order for business cards from an English saleswoman, travelling for a fashion firm, who was passing through Singapore. He was asked to deliver the cards after dinner at the Adelphi Hotel, and when he did so he was invited to go for a drive.

That finished up at an old hotel in a dark compound off Keppel Road; and there, to his astonishment, he found himself being ushered into a discreet bedroom with the lady. He told me he was so surprised that for a moment he did not realise what was happening. "A white woman....." he mused, incredulous at his good fortune.

Nobody in our boarding house was taking out a Eurasian girl, much as they would have liked to — if it could have stopped at that. If there were any survivors among my contemporaries who listened in the 1970s, as I did, to the fascinating B.B.C. series

Plain Tales From The Raj, they would have been as surprised as I was at hearing retired Calcutta merchants recalling with curiously insensitive relish how they treated the "B-class girls", the Anglo-Indian girls, as playthings and sex objects during the six months of the hot weather — and dropped them when the social whirl of the cold season began and they were expected to partner virginal girls from England. I noted with particular envy the recollection of one nabob that those Eurasian girls "sizzled with sex".

No such amusements were possible for the Singapore counterparts of those Calcutta mercantile assistants. For one thing, the strictly brought-up girls of the Eurasian community (mostly from Catholic families) would never have consented to any such degrading treatment; and for another, the loneliest of young European bachelors knew that an affectionate friendship with a self-respecting Eurasian girl could only mean a temporary liaison for him and heartbreak for her.

I can think of much better ways to spend what should be the most magical years of life; but, of course, that was the price that had to be paid for a job in the Far East, anywhere from India to the China Coast; and for army service as well, at that time.

The contrast between that way of life, and what it might have been at Home, was borne strongly upon me when I received a letter several years later from a friend whom I had known in an accountancy job in Singapore, and who left after making a modest pile on the stock market during his first agreement (as was possible during the later 1920s). He was living in an outer-London suburb; he had joined a tennis club and a cycling club. It was a good life, he wrote, and he would never live in Singapore again.

When I thought of those fresh and pretty English girls at the tennis club and on the Sunday cycle excursions, it seemed to me that "going down the line" was pouring the sweet wine of youth down the gutters of Asia. It sounds rhetorical, I know; but it was the truth; and I think the ghosts of Cavenagh Road would agree.

29
Upcountry

AS A GREAT PORT Singapore looked out on the whole world, but on the landward side its Malayan horizon hardly extended beyond the Straits of Johore for the vast majority of its inhabitants. The way of life in all its racial communities and for all classes was still as insular, as introverted, as it had been before the Great War. It is a safe guess that in 1923 nearly everybody in the Asiatic clerical class or middle class had never been off the island — and if the *Straits Times* office was a typical one, that would be true of most of the European community too, for neither Snewin nor Hoppy had ever been in the F.M.S., and I am not sure that Ager had been either.

As the capital of the Straits Settlements Singapore had close ties with its sister Settlements of Penang and Malacca; many family ties too, for the Straits-born and Eurasian communities. As Johore's colonial neighbour, Singapore had a special relationship with that State that went back a century in local history. The reigning Sultan, Sir Ibrahim, was as familiar a figure in the city as his father, Sultan Abu Bakar, had been.

But Singapore people in general knew very little about the rest of Malaya — outside business and official circles, that is to say, and not all of them. For everybody else the "F.M.S." — as the old Federation of Perak, Selangor, Negri Sembilan and Pahang was always referred to — was almost like another country, a remote territory in central Malaya, of no interest to them. As for the Unfederated States in the north, Kedah and Perlis were hardly more than names; Trengganu and Kelantan even more so, since the East Coast beyond Pahang was still inaccessible except by sea.

Of course there had been rail and sea links between Singapore and Malaya for many years. The Johore State Railway completed the southern link in the main line through the Peninsula in 1908, and since 1918 it had been possible to travel by train from Johore Bahru to Bangkok (though I never met anyone who had done it, for travellers to the Siamese capital normally went by sea).

Travel upcountry by rail from Singapore at the time when my memories begin was usually for business reasons, occasionally social or family ones, but never for holidays. Two trains a day left the Tank Road terminus to connect with the day or night mail waiting at Johore Bahru station for Kuala Lumpur — and for practically all intermediate stations on the 250-mile run. Passengers crossed the Straits by the launch ferry operated by the F.M.S. Railways, and that was always a pleasant break in the journey, whether in the freshness of the early morning or in the evening, and especially for travellers arriving on the other side of the Straits after a day or night in the train.

But daytime travel upcountry by train from Singapore was anything but a pleasure. Soot from the soft coal bought by the F.M.S. Railways from Malayan Collieries — at Batu Arang, Selangor — blew in at the window, and one's white suit was grimy by the time the train reached K.L. about six o'clock in the evening. Yet it was so hot in the train that the carriage window had to be left open.

The day mail stopped at all the small wayside stations in the planting districts, and the human interest on the platform and the scenery of the countryside offered some compensation, at least for a city dweller like myself, for the discomforts of the long day in the train. The night mail, in which firstclass passengers got a sleeper (two bunks to a compartment) was more comfortable, but noisy and draughty. That was no pleasure jaunt either.

Travellers who could afford the time much preferred to go by sea to Malacca or Port Swettenham, aboard one of the "little white ships" of the Straits Steamship Company, and thence inland by hire-car or train. However, my recollection of Straits Steamship travel is that the firstclass passengers were almost entirely European. Between the deck passengers and ourselves there were middle-class Asiatics in second-class cabins. In those days very few were so Westernised in speech and habits as to be comfortable in the company of Europeans. The passengers in the first-class dining saloon would almost always be Singapore business or professional men or Government officers.

For other European employees in offices and shops and factories who would have liked to do some sightseeing upcountry by rail or sea, and might have had the money to do it, there was no local leave for anybody, except in the Government service, where the European officers got annual leave in addition to Home leave.

The more senior Tuan Besars of the European business community might get a very occasional holiday at Penang Hill which had just acquired its funicular railway, built by a benevolent Straits Settlement Government — not to benefit the Asiatic residents sweltering in Georgetown, but to make it easier for Europeans to use the hill as a health resort, especially their womenfolk, who were thought to need relief from the heat of the plains. The more affluent Tuan Besars might visit the hill stations of Java or Brastagi in Sumatra perhaps once in their Eastern careers. But, if one reads their reminiscences, it seems to have been as difficult for most of them to get away from their desks in or around Raffles Place as for anybody else.

For the junior men of the European business community in Singapore — "assistants" as we were labelled, when below the managerial level — the only hope of ever enjoying the coolness of Penang Hill was a once-in-a-lifetime leave for a honeymoon or convalescence on doctor's orders. I have to thank an appendicitis operation in 1925 for my first enchanting memories of Penang.

The only other chance of seeing a bit of life upcountry for young men like ourselves was to be picked to represent the S.C.C at Rugby football or soccer, cricket or hockey, against their counterparts in Malacca or Seremban or Kuala Lumpur; and in the Malaya Cup fixtures the top players in the Eurasian and Asiatic clubs might get a weekend upcountry too.

If you worked for one of the few big firms that had branches elsewhere in the Colony or in the F.M.S. (more likely Penang and Malacca), you might spend a year or two in one upcountry town or another. But in my boarding house, in which half a dozen British firms were represented, nobody had even got as far as Johore Bahru; and when I led two of my fellow-boarders up the river to Kota Tinggi and back via Johore Bahru, it was just as much an adventure in exploration for them as it had been for me the first time.

At least we European assistants could look forward to Home leave once every three, four or five years (the term varied with the employer). But the local staff in our offices would never get away from Singapore. For the clerical class — Eurasian, Chinese or Indian — there were only the public holidays: Chinese New Year, Hari Raya, Thaipusam, Christmas, the King's Birthday, and European bank holidays — in all, about a dozen days in the year. In the shops of Chinatown there were literally only three days off in the year — at Chinese New Year — and no weekends either. Sunday for them was just like any other working day.

Seaside or hill holidays in Malaya were not even a dream of the future in Singapore in 1923 — for no-one foresaw what a vast difference the motor road across the Johore Causeway would eventually make. Resorts like Port Dickson and Morib on the West Coast or the beaches of Pahang were only visited by people living in the F.M.S. The new hill station of Fraser's Hill had just been opened up by the Selangor Government — again, frankly for European health reasons, not for general enjoyment — but for European residents of the F.M.S., not those in remote Singapore. The hill bungalows of Maxwell's Hill above Taiping and Bukit Kutu in Selangor would not even have been heard of by anyone who had not lived in the F.M.S.

The more well-to-do residents of Singapore took their seaside holidays at the Government bungalows at Changi, or at many other such bungalows, European and Asiatic, along the Changi and Tanah Merah and Siglap beaches, and even on the Seletar shore, where the Royal Navy and Royal Air Force had not yet disturbed the primeval solitude of the Johore Straits, and where the boats of the Orang Laut, the sea gypsies of Malay race but not Muslim faith, were still to be seen occasionally in the mangrove swamps.

30

The Johore Planters

ON SUNDAY NIGHTS at the old Tank Road railway station there was always a queue of European planters waiting to go back to their rubber estates in Johore after a lively weekend in the city, and many rounds of stengahs, sukus, pahits, gin slings and other varieties of drinks at the Raffles or the Europe. If you saw a jolly rubicund face beneath a double terai hat (a double felt hat with a brim at least two feet in diameter) in Raffles Place on a Saturday morning, that was almost certainly a Johore planter.

One Sunday night I was waiting on the platform at Tank Road to board the night mail for Kuala Lumpur — this must have been after the Causeway was opened for rail traffic in 1923 — when a young planter recognised me as having been with him at Kingswood School, Bath. His name was D.V. Byles, and that encounter led on to a weekend with him on his estate in the Kluang district of Johore. That really was an experience worth recording today, for there was a clearing on the estate where virgin jungle had been felled on contract by Javanese immigrants, and these people were living in makeshift huts between the trunks of huge old trees which they had felled with a little hand-axe. (No bulldozer or power saws in those days). They already had little plots of tapioca — *Ubi Kayu*, the poor man's potato in Malaya — and other vegetables growing in the rich soil, and they were adapting to these primitive pioneering conditions with remarkable contentment and success.

On that Saturday afternoon half a dozen planters from Byles's estate and a neighbouring one gathered at his place for a pigeon shoot. In the hour before sunset the line of guns waited for the *punai,* the green pigeon, as they flashed over a clearing in their regular flight from feeding grounds to roosting place. In that lonely situation it was a scene of outdoor life and sport that helped to explain the attraction of planting life in Malaya for many young men from Britain who would have had a much more prosaic one if they had stayed at Home.

On Sunday the planters gathered again in Byles's bungalow for a curry tiffin — and what a tiffin! Four kinds of curry — pigeon, chicken, beef and hardboiled eggs — prepared by his Indian cook. Before the meal the planters sat around for hours (it was an entirely male group) consuming round after round of drinks — and that hospitality was expensive, even with prices as cheap as they then were. When the Depression came in the early 1930s and many young planters lost their jobs — never to get them back again because their employers had learnt that they did not need an assistant for every four hundred acres — I thought of the money that must have gone down the drain during that Sunday morning in Byles's bungalow, and in hundreds of others from all the way down the Peninsula from Kedah to Johore.

Living was expensive in a lonely situation like that anyway. Byles had been getting a box of Cold Storage food sent up by train from Singapore once a week; but he had found that beyond his means, and was now living on what he could get from the Chinese shop in Kluang, and what his cook brought back from the market when he cycled to the village every morning.

An estate assistant had to attend muster in the Tamil coolie lines at dawn (for the latex will not flow from the rubber trees once the day heats up), and I accompanied Byles there and on his rounds, where he had nothing to do except supervise the tapping and weeding. But that has left an unforgettable memory for me: the beauty of the sun lighting up the wall of virgin jungle around the clearings, and the whooping of the wah-wahs, the little black

THE JOHORE PLANTERS

apes, in the tree-tops, as they always do at dawn but not during the day.

During another weekend with Byles we went to the Government resthouse in Kluang village for a drink — and there, seated on the verandah, all by herself, was a European woman. Byles would not go in! He was so unaccustomed to the society of white women that he could not bring himself to meet one. A Tamil girl from the coolie lines had moved in with him; and you have to know what life was like in a planting district newly opened up for rubber to understand how much difference to a bachelor's life that might make. The convention was that it was all right so long as the girl came from a neighbouring estate; but I suspect that Byles had broken that rule. The temptations were overwhelming, and they were often quite intentionally placed in a young planter's way.

Another memory of Byles is of the suddenness with which a bout of malaria came on. Normally fit in the morning, he was shivering with headache and fever in the afternoon — and that came on regularly once a month, and dosing yourself with quinine because it was no use calling a doctor.

The few British doctors who carried on singlehanded in wide and scattered practice in the planting districts were a particularly fine type, accustomed to treating loneliness as much as physical ills, embodying the human side of medicine as it could not be seen in the waiting rooms of busy doctors in the city. Byles told me that once when ill and very depressed with malaria and complications on another estate, a visit by the South Johore estate doctor left behind a psychological tonic in the bungalow that he had remembered with gratitude ever since.

A mental picture of planting life elsewhere in Johore is of a Saturday when I accompanied the S.C.C. Rugby fifteen to Genuang, an even smaller outstation than Kluang, to play South Johore, a team made up of planters. The game was played on the padang in front of the small district club, the black-and-gold S.C.C. colours making a bright touch of colour on the green field, surrounded on all sides by a dark wall of rubber trees, and it seemed a very English scene in the heart of Johore.

After the game several of us were taken by one of the older planters, in his thirties but still a bachelor, back to his estate for dinner in his vast gloomy bungalow. Our host was a rather queer and introverted personality who had lived a solitary life too long, but we talked about the district, and he told us of a Somerset Maugham situation on another estate in which the manager had come back from Home leave with an English wife, and the former Tamil housekeeper was still on the estate. It was a problem that had not yet surfaced, and the planting community of the district were wondering if and when it would.

After dinner we went back to the Genuang club for a dance. But the only partners for about thirty men were four or five middle-aged wives, and one astonishing vision of beauty, a single girl whose tall and slender figure was sheathed in a ball gown of shimmering green. Alas, the wives looked (and assuredly felt) dumpy and unattractive by comparison with her. She had come out from England to visit relatives and see what life was like on a rubber estate. But the Girl in Green was monopolised all night by two glamorous young army officers in the S.C.C. team, who passed her from one to the other after every dance. The music, by the way, must have been gramophone records, since no-one could play the piano in the lounge. Otherwise it was a melancholy night, with the wives sitting in a glum row by themselves most of the time, and the planters congregated in the bar.

It all ended around midnight with an exodus from the bar and an uproarious procession of planters and their guests marching in the darkness around the bungalow, led by one of the army officers holding up a kerosene lamp and bellowing Home Sweet Home into the Malayan countryside.

31
Rural Rides

GROVE ROAD ..... once an important road, the direct and shortest route to Katong: yet today, not only does it no longer exist, but only the oldest Singaporeans know that it ever existed.

One day I rode out on my motor cycle along Grove Road to interview old Billy Dunman (as he was always known) about some scheme he was involved in as a Municipal Commissioner. Grove Road, after it branched off Geylang Road, ran through a vast mangrove swamp that stretched a mile inland from the Kallang coast. The road here became a long causeway, with steaming mud and tangled black roots on either side at low tide. On the farther side of the swamp was an extensive coconut plantation, protected by a high bund from the deep tidal creek that skirted it; and among the palms was the rambling old residence of its proprietors, a European family that had lived in Singapore through three generations.

Billy Dunman was the grandson of Thomas Dunman, who left his job with a Singapore mercantile firm in 1843 to become the first Commissioner of Police, and who had raised and trained the Settlement's first efficient police force by the time he died in 1871. He was a remarkable character who used to roam Chinatown alone at night, chatting with heads of secret societies, and safe because of his extraordinary personal prestige; so you can imagine the family traditions in that estate bungalow.

The Dunman Estate is an illustration of how close to the city the countryside then was. Another — and a particularly odd one, this — is the snipe swamp that a European lawyer named Richard Page rented farther out at Siglap. He was a wealthy bachelor, one of the senior members of the Bar; and when the snipe arrived on their annual migration from winter in northern Asia he used to invite his friends out to his swamp for a Sunday-morning shoot.

One enchanted night on the Changi Road is my most beautiful memory of rural Singapore. The American Methodist Mission had a bungalow farther along the East Coast where the missionaries and their families could have a seaside holiday, which they could otherwise never have afforded on their meagre incomes, particularly the unmarried American girls working as teachers in the large English-language schools conducted by the mission. (One of them became my wife in later years).

One night when I had been a guest of my American friends at this seaside retreat I rode back to the city, as I had to go to office the next day. It was a perfectly still night of full moon, shining on the coconut palms that formed an endless canopy over the sleeping countryside. There is a magical effect of moonlight on foliage of the Eastern tropics that is not seen in temperate climes, and it was on the feathery fronds of the palms that night.

The road seemed deserted, so rare was it to pass a car at that time of night, and the only sound was the chugging of my little two-stroke Douglas on the soft surface of the laterite road. Half a dozen shophouses at the junction with the Bedok road were the only signs of life, and beyond them the coconut plantations went on for miles in the hilly country along the Changi Road, until it reached the outer suburbs and merged into Upper Geylang Road. The plantations are all gone now, and soon the Changi Road as it was half a century ago will no longer be even a memory.

The inland scenery of Singapore Island presented very few contrasts at that time — nearly all of it being coconuts and rubber — but here is one of them, a memory of Changi itself, following my little epitaph on the old Changi Road. This was before my motor-cycling days, and I was taken out there by the Director of the Botanic Gardens, R.E. Holttum, in his car to join a field excursion of the Singapore Natural History Society. A very senior Government officer, but also living his religion as a Quaker, he was befriending a young newcomer from Home, and, I suppose, also wanted to show him that life in Singapore offered something more than Raffles Place and Cecil Street.

At the end of the Changi Road, beyond the fishing kampong beside the creek, there was a gate, and beyond that a narrow lane through virgin jungle, with grand old trees towering a hundred feet or more on either side. As a botanist (and I think also president of the society), Holttum explained some of its wonders as we walked along, but nothing of that first lesson remains with me now. It was only a small group, twenty or so, mainly European, though I believe the society had one or two Eurasian members as well. It faded away not long after that.

It was all jungle from there on to the coast, and the track led to the two holiday bungalows for Government officers (i.e., European officers). They went back a very long way, or rather, the older one did. "Changi Bungalow has got a lot to answer for," says Roland Braddell in his chapter, "The Merry Past", in the Centenary volumes, "and if the old trees round it could only speak while they are shivering in the night wind they could tell some stories that would make a woman's tiffin party green with envy." He adds that "by 1845 it had become the fashionable place for picnic parties, and by the sixties it was *in excelsis*."

Another and much more extensive tract of jungle survived along the Mandai Road, so this was one of the most popular of country drives. An interesting feature along it was the Seletar hot springs. Fraser and Neave, the soft-drink company, had acquired the property, intending to use the mineralised water some day; and they did in fact bottle and sell it later between the wars. Before that the Singapore Hot Springs Company had had a small factory there, but it was not a commercial success. This was still a pleasant place to stop during a drive, for there were garden paths and shrubs around a small reservoir of fresh water and the disused factory.

Since this is now a rural resort once more for Singaporeans, and the site of their splendid zoo, I cannot resist again going back far beyond my own time, to 1881 and the chronicler of that period, J.T. Thomson. He considered that the finest of the Government bungalows then on the island was the one at Seletar, and this is what he had to say about it:

> "The road leading to it passed for some distance through the thickest of the old forest. At one point, where the road wound through an elevated valley, even in the glare of noonday little more than a subdued twilight reached the traveller as he passed along. The tall forest trees started up from the edge of the road, as straight and regular as the pillars of a colonnade, their branches often meeting at a height of 130 feet overhead.
>
> The bungalow was a simple wooden structure with an attap roof. Fifty yards behind it stood the dark impenetrable jungle, from out of which there gushed a clear, sparkling brook of icy-cold water that ran past the bungalow. This was a very favourite place for bathing and picnics."

Braddell, whom I have to thank for that quotation, adds: "These Government bungalows were built for the East India Company officials, and were, of course, necessary when travel through the island was slow and difficult." That is obviously one of his own family memories, for the East India Company regime had only just ended when his grandfather began to live in Singapore in 1862.

Roland Braddell (later knighted) was born in Singapore and one of the very few European residents who regarded the city as his permanent home. So the reader may like to see how he viewed the scenic changes on the island that I have been recalling. This is what he wrote about it in 1921:

> "It is impossible nowadays to realise the grandeur of the Singapore scenery in the old days, and the above description (Thomson's) has therefore been preserved to give the modern reader some idea of what it was like in the old days. Today most of the roads are flanked by very tired-looking rubber trees, and the scenery is monotonous and often ugly."

And here I am, preserving Thomson's description once again in 1983, and at a time when the contrasts between past and present on the island, as in the city, are becoming more fantastic every year than Braddell and myself ever imagined they would be.

Very different were the island roads that I saw for the first time — for this was a relatively remote and little-known district when I set out on my motor cycle to see the naval base site on the Seletar shore of the Johore Straits.

I remember narrow hilly roads (laterite, of course) winding through rubber estates, a noisy row going on at a Tamil coolie lines among the rubber trees, a planter's bungalow on a hill-top with his private road leading up to it, no traffic whatever after I had left the more populous countryside nearer the city — it might have been a planting district anywhere in the F.M.S.

There were in fact several European estate managers there and elsewhere on the island, living the same kind of life in the same kind of isolated bungalows, as their counterparts upcountry — except that they were fortunate in being so close to the social life of the city, in which they were often seen.

For me that motor-cycle exploration through the dark, regimented, man-made rubber forest was a monotonous one so far as scenery went, but interesting nevertheless when one thought of the traffic that that lonely road from the Johore Straits to the city was going to carry in the not distant future.

My purpose in going out there was to see what work had been

done on the naval base site since the Straits Settlements Government had bought that land from the Bukit Sembawang Rubber Company — a local company whose directors lived in Singapore — and had presented it as a gift to the Imperial Government, as the Colony's contribution to the cost of the base.

But when the road came out of the rubber and reached the Seletar shore, there was nothing to be seen except a new iron fence and a shed. No work going on anywhere, though some rubber trees had been cleared behind the fence. This was after the British Labour Party had won the general election and declared that it would not go on with what Ramsay MacDonald, the new Prime Minister, had denounced in the House of Commons while in Opposition as "the wild and wanton escapade of Singapore". So the Admiralty had as yet left no mark on the Johore Straits except that iron fence.

At the end of the road, on the muddy beach, was a broken-down little wooden jetty, but that had nothing to do with the base, having been there long before any such Imperial intrusion was ever thought of. It was used by country people wanting to be ferried to the islands lying midway in the Straits or to the Johore shore beyond them.

At the end of 1924 the Conservative Party was back in office again, and promptly announced that the Singapore base would be re-activated; but in fact nothing was done until 1928 except clear the ground.

However, rubber enters into my motor-cycling memories much closer to the city than that. When I rode "round The Gap" — as Singapore people called their favourite drive in those days — and crossed the range from the Pasir Panjang side, there were rubber estates all the way to Holland Road and Tanglin — very poor rubber, much of it struggling to survive in the laterite gravel of the hilly land on that side of the island.

But one would have to go no farther out of town than Tanglin Barracks, or just beyond — Swettenham Road and thereabouts — to see a profitable European-owned rubber estate, with its British manager living in an imposing bungalow, two miles from the G.P.O.; and his rubber trees in that valley soil would stand in comparison with any seen upcountry.

At that time there was no housing or other development of any kind on the range of hills around The Gap, and one could enjoy the view of the island coast far below, and the Sembilan Islands and the sea, in silence and solitude. There also was the finest country walk to be had anywhere near the city: along the steep ridge from The Gap to Mount Faber, following a path through bracken and native rhododendron, with a glorious seascape on one side and an island landscape on the other.

32
People And Places

THIS CHAPTER IS JUST a desultory stroll "down memory lane", a journalistic cliche almost too well-worn to use, but one which expresses what I want to do: to pluck from oblivion flashbacks in an old man's brain, each of which is a different glimpse of the Singapore scene as it then was, a little sketch for a documentary of the times.

The Women's Leper Hospital was at the town end of Bukit Timah Road ..... I was taken there one Sunday afternoon by the Rev. Floyd Sullivan, and I can see that dreadful place still. It was as if we were suddenly back in the last century; and that was where this very small and strictly segregated hospital really was.

From the main road we entered a completely bare courtyard (no trees, no garden), surrounded by high walls. In a shelter shed at one side were twenty or thirty women of various races, just sitting there blank and motionless in the afternoon heat, doing nothing whatever, figures of boredom and misery.

Among them, however, there was one brave lady: a Eurasian woman teacher in one of the Methodist girls' schools who had contracted leprosy, and was trying to give her fellow-patients not only the consolation of her own Christian faith, but her own simple forms of occupational therapy, such as a sewing group and study classes, so far as she could on her own at a time when hospital almoners and social welfare services were unknown. The purpose of my missionary friend's visit was to let this lady know that she was not forgotten by her friends outside, but also to conduct a short service for a little group of the women whom she had gathered around her.

Leprosy was regarded with general fear and horror in the Asiatic population. Actually it was not contagious except by prolonged and intimate contact, but one could be sure that that Eurasian patient was the only one who had any visitors. Not only was it incurable, with the drugs then available, but it meant being completely and finally cut off from family and the outside world.

I wrote some impressions of that visit in the *Straits Times,* but whether that had anything to do with the fact that a new women's leper hospital was built in a pleasanter rural situation not long afterwards, I do not know. Where the Men's Leper Hospital was in the city, I never knew. Nor did I ever hear anything more about leprosy in Singapore between the wars; but there were isolation hospitals specially for this disease outside Kuala Lumpur and on Pulau Jerejak, off the coast of Penang; and a more modern hospital for male patients was no doubt built somewhere on Singapore Island too.

An excursion of purely sightseeing interest for which I have to thank my friend Sullivan was to Kampong Roko, on the other side of the Kallang basin, one of the most curious centres of Malay life as it then went on in the network of rivers, creeks and swamps on that side of Singapore.

It was called Kampong Roko because many of its inhabitants earned their living by making the native cheroots, but it also had a reputation as an almost impenetrable hideout of smugglers; and I understood why as soon as we landed from the sampan we had taken across the Kallang River from the Beach Road side. The whole kampong was built out over the water, and it was a maze of high plank paths between the houses. However, none of the inhabitants showed any resentment at this intrusion of two Europeans looking around at their homes and the marine way of life in them. Kampong Roko vanished when the Kallang airport,

Singapore's first, was constructed halfway between the wars.

Sullivan had an inexhaustible interest in Asiatic Singapore, both Chinese and Malay, and was fluent in the languages required to explore both of those quarters. I am indeed fortunate to have known him, and to be able to draw upon his vast fund of local knowledge for these recollections. It is to him I am indebted for Chinatown memories of an old-style Chinese medicine shop (an astonishing experience, when your guide knows what he is looking at — including a bullock's penis, whose medicinal value needs no explanation); and for a peep inside a Government opium saloon, where coolies reclining on dirty wooden bunks were enjoying the pipe that was their only pleasure in life, and the pipe-dreams that went with it.

I must be one of the last living persons who remember the old General Hospital, built in 1882 but added on to several times since. Oldtimers would have recalled when all the nursing there was done by sisters from the Convent. That ended in 1900, when the first professional nursing sisters were brought out from Britain; but so great was the turnover then and even afterwards that the Principal Medical Officer of the Colony (also in the F.M.S.) complained that he was "running a marriage bureau".

Anyone who had to have a major operation after the Great War would go to Java if he could afford it, for the Dutch surgeons of Batavia and Sourabaya had a much higher reputation than those in Singapore. However, not long after I arrived two British surgeons of Harley Street standard were brought out, and those fears soon disappeared.

My first visit to the old General Hospital was to see someone in the "European ward", which was a separate one-storey block of timber construction, with very pleasant, quiet rooms and an outside verandah open to the greenery and sunshine outside. That was where Conrad was once a patient, for there is an unmistakable impression of it in one of his stories.

After the new General Hospital was built on the same site I myself was a patient for an appendicitis operation, and all the others in that long ward were still Europeans. Where the Asiatic patients were, especially those capable of paying for equivalent accommodation, I do not know. The Tan Tock Seng Hospital in Moulmein Road was still referred to in Medical Department terminology as "a pauper hospital".

At about the same time I had to go to the Medical College at the back of the General Hospital on some reporting enquiry, and what I remember about that is the depression of the Principal, Dr McAlister, over the absolute refusal of his superior, the head of the Medical Department, to allow any funds for research.

The Medical College was then the only institution of tertiary education in Singapore — or anywhere in Malaya — and remained so until the second decade between the wars. The official policy at that time was to keep the College strictly for the training of a junior medical service (which it did for the F.M.S., as well as the Straits Settlements). None of the Eurasian, Chinese, Indian or Ceylonese doctors who qualified there could hope for promotion to the higher level of their profession in Government hospitals anywhere in Malaya, that being a preserve of the European doctors, who came from the famous medical schools of Edinburgh, Dublin and London.

However, later in the decade half a dozen Singapore graduates were admitted to specialist posts in the Colony, though the Chinese and Indian members of the Legislative Council complained bitterly that promotion was only for those of "a European cast of countenance" (in other words, Eurasians) — which in fact it was.

Within those limits, the King Edward VII College of Medicine had had a very good record since it was established in 1905 (the Straits Settlements Government having sent its medical students to Madras before that); and since 1916 the L.M.S. of Singapore had been recognised by the General Medical Council of Great Britain as a qualification for what was then known as "the Colonial List of the Medical Register".

My only other memory of the Medical College comes much later in my career between the wars, but unfortunately only at secondhand; it comes from the attractive Eurasian girl who was then the editor's secretary in Cecil Street, and who told me that the medical students entertained their visitors by taking them up to the top floor, where they could gaze down on the European nursing sisters strolling about stark naked in their quarters below — no doubt their way of relaxing after a day in the wards.

A pleasant custom that had been going on since the horse-and-carriage days was the band concert that was given in the Botanic Gardens once a month, on the Sunday night nearest to full moon, by the regimental band from Tanglin Barracks. This was the only outdoor social occasion on which you might see the European and Eurasian communities represented together (only those, however, as the Asiatic communities as yet scarcely ever frequented the Botanic Gardens at any time during the year). The cars would be parked on the approach roads leading up to the bandstand, people would be strolling about, and on a fine moonlight night it could be delightful.

While this was going on, there was in the Botanic Gardens a solitary and remarkable survivor of the primeval Singapore: a huge old turtle that lived at the bottom of the lake, and was seen occasionally by the gardeners. How old he was nobody could even guess, but he was certainly contemporaneous with the virgin jungle nearby, the only patch of the original jungle left in suburban Singapore — and still carefully preserved there.

Elsewhere on the island the last of the sambhur deer survived in the Bukit Timah jungle (and not long before that there had been a few of the smaller kijang deer too). There were also wild pig in the swamps of the West Coast, and a few city dwellers pursued the sport of pig-shooting out there. All that wild life on the island became extinct between the wars (including the Gardens' turtle).

The Botanic Gardens were then as well-kept and expertly managed as they are now, but if any Singaporean of today could go back and see them as they were in the 1920s he would be surprised at the absence of many familiar shrubs and flowers.

There were many new importations for the amateur gardener, and for the colourful Chinese plant nurseries, between the wars.

But the most important importation of all, the wild Hevea rubber tree of the Amazon jungles, had come before the turn of the century, and the botanist responsible for it, H.N. Ridley, was very much a living memory in the Gardens, for he was still living in England in his eighties and actively collaborating with his successor, R.E. Holttum. The last of the original rubber trees — received from Kew Gardens via Ceylon — from which Ridley distributed the first seeds of two million acres of plantation rubber in Malaya were still growing in what had been an extension of the Botanic Gardens, the experimental gardens on Bukit Timah Road. They disappeared when the site was cleared for Raffles College.

Oldham Hall, which was approached by Oldham Lane off Orchard Road, was the boys' boarding school of the American Methodist Mission. I lived there for a while, and the memory of it that I want to recall, as a sidelight on the times, is of a four-storey building crammed with schoolboys, and no sewerage, no flush toilets, whatsoever. I shared a bathroom, provided with two or three wooden jambans, with two American missionary teachers, and the conditions in it were frequently unspeakable. So what the boys must have had to put up with can be imagined.

Oldham Hall was the place where the United States Consulate rid themselves of the occasional American stranded in Singapore for one reason or another, whom they had no funds to help. It was no part of the Methodist Mission's activities to act as a welfare agency for the U.S. Consulate, but when confronted with destitute fellow-countrymen Sullivan was always too compassionate to say No.

A few years later Oldham Hall was demolished, and the boarders were moved to a huge old house named Dunearn, beyond Chancery Lane, which was then the limit of suburban development on that side of Bukit Timah Road. Dunearn was another interesting place, for it was built by a German Consul-

General in the last century as his official residence, and the extensive grounds sloping down to Dunearn Road had preserved the family's mangosteen orchard.

Oldham Lane is still there: a name that commemorates Bishop Oldham, who was an English officer in the Indian Army when he resigned to become a missionary and one of the founders of the Methodist Mission in Singapore. He was an exceptionally eloquent and moving preacher, and the only one who ever saw a Governor of the Colony in his congregation at Wesley Church — Sir Arthur Young, the Governor before and during the Great War.

The site of Dunearn is now occupied by the Anglo-Chinese School in fine modern buildings constructed since the World War; and I hear that the Methodist boys' and girls' schools have both started to go co-ed — an innovation that would have been unthinkable during the years we are now recalling, when the Chinese girls attending the M.G.S. on Mount Sophia arrived in rickshaws chaperoned by the family amah.

The headmistress and senior staff of Raffles Girls' School in Victoria Street were recruited in England, and they maintained a snooty detachment from their counterparts in the American mission schools (who were equally, if not better, qualified.) The headmistress, Miss Buckle, was prominent in the Singapore social scene in those days, noted particularly for using a cigarette holder about 15 inches long.

The headmistress of the junior school in that new building was a victim of the extraordinary colour prejudice of those days. She moved in European circles for some years, but then it became known that far back in her family history there was a Eurasian connection, and she was no longer invited by former friends. The whisper was that certain Government officers had hinted at "a touch of the tar-brush" — surely the most abominable sneer ever heard in European society in British Malaya as in British India, but much more rarely and less unkindly in French Indochina or the Dutch East Indies.

A happier story of Raffles Girls' School in Stamford Road is of the Eurasian teacher known as "Aunt Nettie". She was a Miss Buxton, the daughter of a sea-captain; and when the British came back after the World War she was awarded the O.B.E. for brave and dangerous deeds during the Japanese occupation. What they were I never knew, or have forgotten. What a story it would make today!

The Rhio Archipelago ..... that is the last memory you might expect to find in this chapter, or indeed from any British resident in Singapore between the wars, for it was as much foreign territory then as it is now. A visa from the Dutch Consul in Singapore was necessary, and hard to get, for Dutch officialdom was naturally suspicious about the motives of any British resident wanting to explore beyond that line of islands on the other side of the Singapore Strait.

However, the American Methodist Mission had a purely non-political outpost in the Archipelago, having stationed a Chinese pastor there whose stipend was paid from Singapore; and when the Rev. Floyd Sullivan sought permission as district superintendent to go there he got his visa, and one for me too, had the Dutch consulate known that the second application was for no missionary but a *Straits Times* reporter, it might not have been so easy.

The Malays have — or had then — a saying that the islands of the Rhio Archipelago are as countless as "a gantang of pepper berries", and that is my impression too. The extraordinary part of that trip, in one of the little Chinese-owned steamers that anchored off Johnston's Pier, was the navigation: continually turning and twisting between the islands with no landmarks other than those in the steerman's memory, sometimes a sudden right-angle turn into a deep green channel so narrow that one could have thrown a stone on to the islands on either side.

Our destination was a large Chinese village deep inside the Archipelago — a surprising discovery in this Indonesian territory. It was large enough to have a Dutch controleur stationed there (Eurasian, I think). But the village had this regular steamer service to Singapore, and that was its market for the dried fish, charcoal burnt in the mangrove swamps and other products which this isolated Chinese community produced. The steamer went on from there to complete its trading itinerary in the islands.

The Chinese pastor had only a very small flock, which I saw when we attended a service in his wooden church, no larger than a European bungalow. My own outlook was really a secular one, for I had never gone back to the faith of my fathers with my Methodist friends, but it was moving to hear the hymns and scriptures of Christianity in this remote little congregation that could not speak a word of English.

However, the service was in one of the Chinese vernaculars; it was very hot inside the church; and I have to confess that I fell asleep. This lapse in what the congregation must have supposed to be a junior missionary from Singapore must have made a bad impression; but Sullivan was sympathetic and did not reproach me.

We stayed overnight and took the same steamer back to Singapore the next day. Ever since then I have known what a marvellous natural playground lies at Singapore's front door if only political barriers can be overcome.

In the police courts I knew a senior inspector named Farquhar who was a survivor of the days when European sergeants and constables were seen on beat duty in the city streets. They wore a blue khaki uniform, which must have been extremely hot. "Many a man have come off the beat and gone straight to bed — too tired to eat," Farquhar once told me.

The European contingent was first recruited in 1881, the idea being to set an example of discipline and esprit de corps for the Indian and Malay police; but there were constant grievances over pay and other conditions, and in 1906 the sergeants and constables were either sent Home or promoted. Since then there had been no European officers below the rank of inspector.

I knew a young officer of the Malayan Civil Service named T.B. Cocker, and I have always remembered him saying: "I chose the M.C.S. because it is the only white service left". It struck me at the time as a strangely narrow-minded approach to a career that would be spent in an Asiatic multi-racial society, and a surprising one too, for his tolerant personal philosophy derived from the Greek and Latin classics, which he was still reading in the old fashioned residential hotel in Stamford Road where he was living when I met him.

Racialist, the catchword of today, was never heard at that time. What the non-European communities of the Colony talked about was the colour bar in Government and commercial employment at the executive level; but that was the only time I ever heard it privately but forthrightly declared as the reason for choosing the Malayan Civil Service from a variety of other options open to university graduates passing the Colonial Service competitive examinations at Home. My own guess would be that in that respect my friend Cocker was not typical of most of his contemporaries.

Cocker would certainly never have shown any such underlying racialism in his official dealings with the local communities; but he never had a chance to do so anyway, for when he went Home on leave he failed in his Bar examinations and committed suicide. He had been specialising in the legal branch of the M.C.S., and I suppose he could not bring himself to come back after that.

33

The New Boy

MY THEME IS SINGAPORE, not myself, except in so far as it has to be a personal story; and the junior reporter on his rickshaw rounds does seem to have been making some objective mental notes that may have some interest for posterity. But the very young and callow Englishman in the European business community of Raffles Place is also part of the story.

I felt very much the new boy in the colonial school — and that is more than just a metaphor, for the other European assistants in mercantile offices and banks whom I used to see in Raffles Place in the tiffin hour were nearly all from the lesser public schools of England and Scotland; and their interests, values and taboos were remarkably like those drilled into me at Kingswood School, Bath. There was the same sexual segregation too, as in those semi-monastic dormitories. The excessive importance of Rugby football in what was sometimes described as a cultural desert makes me think that in that respect we were not quite grown-up. I once heard a rugged character named Dr Lindow, who refereed the Malaya Cup games, declare: "Rugby football is my religion." And that when he was going Home on retirement from Government service at fifty-five!

Everybody in Raffles Place was identified by the name-tag of his firm, so to speak, if not by his own name. You might not know who somebody was, but you would know that he was with

Brinkmann's or Barlow's or whatever; and as there were only about twenty firms (apart from shops), the *Straits Times* new boy would be noticed at once, just as he had been during his first days in the junior school.

Most of those young men lived in boarding houses as I did, but those who worked in banks and in several of the larger firms lived in houses provided by their employers — an unsatisfying mess-life with the same people you had been working with all day, and with meals supplied by Cookie on a monthly contract (and naturally making as much out of it as he could for himself).

Looking back on my contemporaries in old age, one thing that interests me is the family ties with Singapore that were represented in Raffles Place. Browsing in the Centenary volumes, I keep coming upon names I knew then as young European bachelors, but whose fathers had been there before them; and there were a few third-generation names as well.

One odd memory of Raffles Place is that the waistcoat appeared to be the sartorial preserve of the Tuan Besar, since nobody else wore it in that climate. But that is one of few contributions I can make to the mythology of the Tuan Besars, who figure so largely in the curiously hostile caricatures of life in colonial Singapore that we see films and novels today. The only other thing I knew about them was that as the most senior men of that mercantile community they went to the Singapore Club for tiffin; and I suppose the circle of my friends and acquaintances in the "G.H." cafe at the same hour hoped to go there one day too.

Even here we are not at the lowest level in Raffles Place. Below us were the European shop assistants in John Little's, Robinson's and Whiteaway Laidlaw's. They started on $250 a month on their first agreement, and on that they could only afford the very cheapest and most squalid boarding houses, and they could have had practically nothing left over for recreation. When I got to know one of them I was reminded of a comment I heard from a shop assistant before I left London. When he learnt that I was going out to Singapore he told me that he had been with Robinson's for four years. "It's a good life for those at the top," he said. "But not for those at the bottom." Now I knew what he meant.

Empress Place on the other side of the Singapore River, the headquarters of the Straits Settlements Government, was as yet known to me only as a reporter; but we should take a look at it too, because the Government officers in the Colonial Secretariat and the Treasury, and in the departments controlled from there formed a separate group within the European community which identified with the Colony as a whole rather than with the mercantile Singapore of Raffles Place and Collyer Quay.

A few had been seconded to one or other of the Unfederated States, but most of them had served in the Straits Settlements throughout their careers. Their memories were of the padi plains and sugar estates of Province Wellesley, the Settlement of Penang (Georgetown and Prince of Wales's Island, as it appeared on the maps), and Malacca and its rural hinterland, with Customs barriers at the borders of Johore and Negri Sembilan.

The Colony and the F.M.S. had their own separate Government departments, and they had had their own civil services up to 1920, when these were merged into the Malayan Civil Service. That was the first pan-Malayan reform, but it was extended to nearly all European Government officers later in this period.

There was yet another and even more separate group within the European community — the Harbour Board engineers, shipyard mechanics, wharf superintendents and their families who had their own club and golf course and their own suburb on the hills behind Tanjong Pagar and Keppel Harbour. From the Raffles Place viewpoint it seemed like a remote and private area, one into which I never penetrated in all my career on the *Straits Times*. In fact, I only once met any European residents from there, and that was an English Methodist family that attended Wesley Church.

* * *

The oldtimers of the European commercial community seemed

to be a different breed from the younger men who had arrived since the 1914 - 18 war. Ager once told me that in his early years, when pay was low, there was no road across the Johore Straits, and there might be long periods between Home leave, you had to make your own interests in the city and on the islands; and one could see the after-effects of that in the way in which these older Europeans identified with Singapore as their home town — even though they took eventual retirement at Home for granted — and particularly in the active interest they took in civic affairs.

At meetings of the Municipal Commissioners they spoke of "the town" when Singapore was already plainly a city, comparable in the region only with Batavia and Bangkok; but they remembered when it was indeed the "old Eastern town" of the Conrad stories, with only half the population of postwar years.

The senior merchants who represented the Singapore Chamber of Commerce in the Legislative Council were wont to speak of "the Settlement", as if we were back in the Singapore left behind by Sir Stamford Raffles in the early nineteenth century. But they had grown up in the Raffles tradition, and that was still strong in the British commercial community of the early 1920s — so much so that it was one of the first things that struck newcomers of the postwar generation.

I never quite knew what those Singapore merchants meant by "the Settlement" in Council debates, but it seemed to relate to Government policy as distinct from civic affairs, particularly when they were defending the free-port policy of Raffles against new import duties to protect Lancashire against the flood of much cheaper piecegoods coming in from Japan.

So the Raffles tradition was still a force in public affairs; but it was also a living tradition in the city as a whole. I remember a cartoon in *Straits Produce,* a local monthly magazine and a witty and sophisticated imitation of *Punch*, that depicted a rickshaw puller in his wide coolie hat gaping openmouthed at a tourist who had just told him to go to Raffles, and demanding to know "which Raffles". There followed a verbal outburst of a dozen places and institutions that bore the name of the founder.

However, neither the social conscience nor the local patriotism that were so genuinely manifested in these colonial Singaporeans had any influence when it came to opium and income tax. Income tax had been imposed as a war tax, and after the war the Colony Government wanted to retain it, because the opium revenue was going to go under pressure from the League of Nations and the Colonial Office sooner or later, and because another source of revenue would be needed anyway to meet growing demands for social progress and other development. But the European community would have none of it. At a mass meeting held in Singapore in 1922 the campaign against income tax reached its climax, and the Straits Government bowed to the storm.

The older European residents were still chuckling over that victory when I arrived, and one refrain that the newcomer constantly heard at that time was this: "The Chinese merchants and shopkeepers kept two sets of books: one for the tax man and one for themselves. The Europeans on a fixed salary had no hope of evading the tax." And that was undeniably true.

However, the tax was just as unpopular with the Chinese business community, who resented Government officers prying into their affairs, and the Chinese Chamber of Commerce backed the European chamber and other public bodies on this issue.

At the same time, the fact that the Colony got nearly a third of its revenue from opium did not seem to trouble the senior Europeans in the least. The Government had a monopoly of the import of opium, and of the dark and squalid saloons in Chinatown where it was retailed to addicts.

This seemed quite startling and shocking to me as a newcomer, but Ager dismissed any such idealistic fallacies by telling me that an Opium Commission had made a thorough study of this habit in Singapore some years before the war, and three British doctors with long local experience had testified from their observation of Chinese patients that opium smoking in moderation was not at all harmful.

Ager firmly believed that the Chinese were just as entitled to their whiffs of opium as he was to his pipe of tobacco and his whisky-and-soda; and in that comfortable conviction I am sure he was typical of his generation. If he had known what we know about cigarette smoking today, he might well have argued that the opium pipe was actually less harmful.

Moreover, when the Colony Government argued that even with the opium revenue a peace-time income tax was necessary to finance social welfare, the senior ranks of the European community simply refused to believe it; and the Chinese and Indian merchant businessmen were only too glad to agree with them. Alas, in hindsight, we know that they were wrong.

34

The Establishment

BEFORE WE SAY a final goodbye to Singapore as it was after the Great War, we should look at the European community of that time, for although I was only a very junior member of it, and still seeing only the surface of expatriate life and society — a term, by the way, never heard there until after the World War — some of those first impressions come back now as revealing echoes of the period.

The newcomer from Home in Raffles Place — and I suppose in Empress Place and the Harbour Board enclave too — found himself at the bottom of a social pyramid at the top of which was the Governor, and beneath him what would now be called the Establishment — another term never heard in those days, but nonetheless very much a reality in colonial society.

His Excellency the Governor of the Straits Settlements, who also had the honorific title of Commander-in-Chief, was in his other role High Commissioner for the Malay States, and British Agent for Sarawak, the independent Sarawak of the White Rajahs, and British North Borneo, a territory owned and administered by the last of the great chartered companies of British mercantile history — in its last days, however, for it was no longer making money for its shareholders.

But the Governor was by no means a figurehead. He left day-to-day administration to his Colonial Secretary, but he had reserve powers of completely autocratic intervention, and not infrequently used them. In the ceremonial and symbolic aspects of his high office the Governor was accorded universal deference and loyalty, but he was by no means free from criticism of his policies in the European community.

The governor when I arrived was Sir Laurence Guillemard, K.C.M.G. (and a lot of other letters after his name). The Colonial Office had evidently decided that what the Colony and the F.M.S. needed in this new period after the war was a financial expert, and so they had sent out to Government House in Singapore a high official of the Treasury in London who was also of course a member of the Home Civil Service. Inevitably he met with prejudice and resentment from a European community, Official and Unofficial, accustomed to expect a new Governor with colonial experience in Africa or elsewhere in the British Empire.

Moreover, Sir Laurence Guillemard had come out with instructions from the Colonial Office to do what he could to meet the grievances of the Sultan of Perak and other Malay Rulers about the Federal bureaucracy that was spreading like an octopus from Kuala Lumpur into the four States of the old Federation.

This had involved him in a feud with Sir George Maxwell, who as Chief Secretary was the executive head of the F.M.S. Government, and who was personally very popular in Singapore, having served there during the war. Sir George Maxwell was one of the ablest and finest officers that the Malayan Civil Service had produced, and himself the son of one of the early British Residents in what were then known as the Native States.

The opposition to the new High Commissioner's proposed reforms in the F.M.S. was so great that he was not able to achieve much; but that was the beginning of a very long and continuous story of British policy in the Malay States that has ended with the Sultans of Perak, Selangor, Negri Sembilan and Pahang being as influential and privileged as they are in the Peninsular Malaysia of today.

There had only been one Governor in Singapore whose entire experience had been in Malaya, and that was Sir Frank Swettenham, who ended his historic Anglo-Malayan career there in 1903. Sir Laurence Guillemard, however, was not the first Governor who did not come from the Colonial Service. Sir John Anderson, who occupied Government House from 1904 to 1911, was also a member of the Home Civil Service, but he had had wide experience in the Colonial Office; and his seniority there was such that when King George V and Queen Mary visited Singapore as Prince and Princess of Wales during their world tour in the S.S. *Ophir* in 1902 he was on board as the Colonial Office representative.

* * *

At the top of the colonial hierarchy, beneath "H.E." — as the Governor was always known in Empress Place — and never mentioned without those potent capital letters in the news columns of the *Straits Times* — was the Colonial Secretary, a formidable figure and very much the old-style colonial autocrat named Sir Frederick James. He had come from West Africa in 1916 — one of those moves from a country where an official had specialised local knowledge to one where he had none, that were constantly going on in the British colonial empire (an empire in itself within the British Empire), scattered over all the continents and oceans of the world except Antartica, and all controlled from the Colonial Office in London.

The Colonial Treasurer ranked next in Empress Place — but in the Treasury his No. 2 was an embittered officer of the Malayan Civil Service, E.L. Talma, who could rise no higher (or so it was believed in the European community of the time) because he was a Ceylon Tamil. He had entered the M.C.S. via the competitive examination held for the Colonial Service as a whole, but there was now a rule that all candidates for cadets appointed to the Straits Settlements or the F.M.S. must be of "pure European birth on both sides". To find the explanation for that, you would have to go to the Malay States rather than the Colony.

Below "the Heaven-born" — a nickname for the civil service

imported from British India, and given to them because they were superior to everybody else in status, authority and society as well — were the heads of Government departments: the Principal Medical Officer, the Inspector-General of Police, the Colonial Engineer, the Director of Education and so on. The three judges were of course also members of the Establishment — but there again, in the Supreme Court building in Empress Place was another embittered man, Mr Justice Sproule, who had been denied promotion, so he believed himself, to Chief Justice of the Straits Settlements because he was a Ceylon burgher, although fully qualified for that high office.

The Bishop of the Church of England (but not the Roman Catholic bishop of the French Mission and its cathedral in Bras Basah Road, still less the American Methodist bishop of Wesley Church in Fort Canning Road) was a member of the Establishment as well, for the Church of England was as much the Established Church in colonial Singapore, in influence if not in any ordinance, as it was at Home. The Colony Government paid the salary of the Colonial Chaplain, otherwise known as the Archdeacon; Bishopsbourne, in the suburban byroad called Bishopsgate (off Jervois Road), was one of the places at which you were expected to call if you had to perform the complete card-dropping ritual; and St. Andrew's Cathedral was where services of special significance in the public life of Singapore were always held.

On the Unofficial side, the members of the Establishment, and perhaps even more conservative and conventional than those that we have been glancing at on the other side, were the Tuan Besars of Raffles Place: the heads of the leading British firms, old-established import and export houses with names that were the stuff of local history: Boustead's, Guthrie's, Paterson Simon's, Adamson Gilfillan, Mansfield's, Sime Darby and the rest.

They were authoritative and powerful figures more powerful behind the scenes in the Legislative Council and at Government House than in their public life; and their power base, so to speak, was the Singapore Chamber of Commerce i.e. the European chamber, as distinct from the Chinese Chamber of Commerce, which was definitely a lesser body, though one which the Colony Government had to treat with respect, and a still lesser one, the Indian Chamber of Commerce. Two other prominent figures in European commercial life were the Chairman and Chief Engineer of the Singapore Harbour Board, and the general manager of the Straits Trading Company, which bought all the tin-ore mined in the F.M.S. for its smelters on Pulau Brani and at Penang.

But, you may well ask, is that a complete sketch of the Establishment at that time? Were not the old Eurasian families (several of them quite well-to-do), and the Chinese millionaire class (already a numerous one), represented at the topmost level of social influence and Big Business? Was there no Old Boy network of vested interests except in one racial community?

Well, perhaps I can answer that indirectly by pointing to the Legislative Council of the Colony as it was in the year before I arrived. The Unofficial side of that body was still as it had been in the last century. The Europeans had eight seats — to say nothing of the Official phalanx on the other side of the chamber — but there was only one Chinese member, and the Eurasian, Indian and Malay communities were not represented at all. If the legislature of the Straits Settlements — Singapore, Penang, Malacca and Province Wellesley — was practically a European body, what else would you expect the Establishment in the capital of the Colony to be?

Council reform came later in 1922. The Chinese now had three seats, and the other communities one each. The Malay seat was vacant for some time while the Government looked for a community leader with sufficient command of English to occupy that seat. But on the Unofficial side the European members were still in the majority, and although the fixed Official majority was abolished, the Governor had the casting vote. It was still a noteworthy reform, however, as the Chinese in Penang and Malacca were now represented as well as those in Singapore; and the new Eurasian, Indian and Malay members began to play a prominent part in the public life of Singapore.

* * *

It will perhaps be apparent already that the European community, official and unofficial, was so divided and so scattered that it was hardly a community at all, except in the racial sense and the colonial situation. But in that sense could be included in the European community the British garrison.

They lived an even more separate life in even more scattered establishments, and we never saw anything of them, except perhaps on the sports field — or in the Government House Circular, in which the more senior officers of the Services and their wives often appeared as dining there with their more senior counterparts in the white civilian community.

First in traditional precedence, but scarcely more than a minimum presence in the port, was the Royal Navy, represented by one officer, known as the Senior Naval Officer, who could have had only a very small office and staff, for the only naval establishment he had to look after was the Admiralty oil wharf at Keppel Harbour. Otherwise he could only have been busy when ships of the China Squadron or the East Indies Squadron — terms that were echoes of the old sailing navy in Eastern seas and still in use — came from Hong Kong, or Trincomalee in Ceylon, to show the flag in Malayan waters.

There was a British infantry battalion at Tanglin Barracks, and a few other small army units: the Royal Garrison Artillery manning the forts, now completely obsolete, on Blakang Mati, (so called The Back of Death because there had been a Malay burial ground there in pre-colonial times, and now called Sentosa — Peace — to mark the change from harbour defences to pleasure resort); the Royal Engineers and the Royal Army Ordnance Corps on Pulau Brani; and the headquarters staff of Malaya Command on Fort Canning, still in barracks which had not changed since Government Hill became a fort in the sixties of the last century.

And that was all there was of the British Army when Singapore had no importance for Great Britain and the British Empire except as a commercial port and the capital of a Crown colony, and when the garrison was consequently only for local defence. As for the Royal Air Force, it was not represented at all, for in 1923, and for several years longer, there was not an airfield on the island.

35
History In The Files

HALF A CENTURY LATER, when I was revisiting Singapore, and went to the library in Times House to look at the *Straits Times* files of my first year or two in the old office in Cecil Street, I was rewarded with some forgotten and eloquent echoes of the city in that chapter of its social history after the Great War. This, for example, from the *Straits Times* of 1923:

> *"Seventeen years ago the motor-bus got properly to work in London, and it got to Singapore three years ago; and it is going to be a huge godsend, though it depends a lot on more and wider roads. Already work-people who can only afford a few dollars a month in rent are leaving Bencoolen Street and taking up wood-shanty houses at Siglap, but doing their day's work in Bencoolen Street."*

That is from the Singapore Improvement Trust report for 1923. It is no wonder that the Trust town-planners were glad to record that new trend when one reads what they had to say about Chinatown at that time.

> *"The density of the Singapore (Chinatown slum) blocks is a record — in two typical blocks recently*

investigated, respectively 555 and 728 inhabitants per acre per night. But there is also a separate and considerable day population, the same cubicles being used by different people day and night ..... this unprecedented overcrowding in dark and disease-saturated old slums is of a record bad type."

Those pioneer British town-planners in Singapore — remember that the Improvement Trust had only been founded in 1918 — had had previous experience of the Calcutta slums, and they went on to say: "The Singapore slums are the worst in the world of which definite knowledge is extant (not excluding the poorest conditions in Calcutta and Bombay.)"

The Improvement Trust at first was concerned only with town-planning, and had neither legal powers nor funds to start re-housing the slum-dwellers.

In those days the Municipal Health Department used to put out a weekly report, and after those insights into Chinatown it is not surprising to find tuberculosis invariably heading the four main killing diseases in Singapore — the others being pneumonia, beri-beri and dysentery, in that order. Beri-beri was a vitamin-deficiency disease caused by the rice diet of the Chinese coolie class.

On the credit side, there was in those *Straits Times* files an echo of a different health menace in the period before the Great War that had been almost forgotten in my time. That was the malaria wave which swept over the city every year, generally reaching its maximum in May, and which raised the death-rate to 85.25 per mille in July, 1911, the worst year on record.

This was recalled at a conference held by the Far Eastern Association of Tropical Medicine in Singapore to mark the 25th anniversary of Sir Ronald Ross's discovery in Calcutta that it was the anopheles mosquito which was the carrier of the malaria parasite (all sorts of fantastic theories about the causes of the fever having been current before that.)

Sir Malcolm Watson, of Klang, Selangor, a pioneer of malaria control on F.M.S. rubber estates — where the death rate among Tamil coolies on certain notorious estates had actually reached 300 per thousand — told the conference how he was called in to advise on similar plans for Singapore in 1911, and of their increasing success, thanks mainly to the Municipality's energetic and outspoken Health Officer, Dr P.S. Hunter (one of the finest figures of my time).

By 1923 there were six square miles of suburban Singapore under mosquito control, and the annual malaria wave was a thing of the past — but only inside those suburbs, as Dr Hunter told the conference. "The wave will not disappear," he said, "until the work in Singapore is completed and until the surrounding countryside ceases to dump its sick on the city." So most of rural Singapore was still as unhealthy as it had ever been.

If that is hard to believe in the Singapore of today, what about this!

> *"A road bus in which I was riding was hailed at Jardine's Steps by a beribboned member of the Royal Engineers. The person in question walked to the front of the bus with his small cane in his hand, and ordered the occupant of the seat beside the driver to get out and go inside. This occupant was a decent middle-aged Malay woman who had boarded the bus at Pasir Panjang and paid her fare."*

That letter in the *Straits Times* was signed "An Englishwoman", and I am glad to add that the heading which the editor put on it was "Arrogance".

Here is a British colonial view of the potential for an Asiatic intelligentsia in 1923:

> *"There has been some talk here as to the formation of a university. I ask you to disabuse your minds of*

> *any such dream. There are not enough boys in Singapore and the Straits — boys who would be thought proper for a university education — to fill the smallest college in Oxford or Cambridge."*

That was Sir Walter Shaw, Chief Justice of the Straits Settlements, addressing the Singapore Teachers' Association.

The more curious and amusing item that turned up in my rummaging among the old files is the opening sentence of the *Straits Times* leader for April 23, 1923:

> *"When one reads the proceedings of the House of Commons and realises that a great English constituency is represented by a vulgar loud-mouthed fellow like George Lansbury ....."*

There we see what a remote place Singapore then was, how incredibly behind the times its British colonial types were with regard to fundamental changes taking place in their own homeland after the Great War. Any such editorial comment would have been unthinkable in that year, but it provoked no criticism from *Straits Times* readers.

When I left England the first Labour members had just won seats in the House of Commons, the first workingmen in what had been a preserve of the upper class; and yet so able an editor as A.W. Still could not realise that they represented a new political force and social challenge of the greatest significance.

Elsewhere in those files, however, you will see why Singapore was such a remote place, why the Far East seemed so much farther in those days.

The mails were sent in advance to Suez, where they were picked up by steamers which had sailed from England before the letters were posted.

In alternate weeks the mails were brought direct to Singapore from Suez by P. and O., or they went to India first and were brought on by British India steamers to Penang, where they were unloaded and sent on to Singapore by train. A typical London mail in 1923, taken from the files, was dispatched on March 29 and arrived on April 22.

A sign of the times was the formation of the Singapore Radio Society in 1923, but its members were interested only in wireless telegraphy and telephony, not broadcasting. The first experimental broadcast of opera by the B.B.C. from Covent Garden had taken place only the previous year.

There are some remarkable glimpses of life upcountry in the files. For example, this item in *Notes from Muar*:

> "The planters in the Muar district had worried of late by the presence of man-eating tigers. During the last year, on one estate under European management, eight coolies have been eaten, and one coolie was taken while tapping within a few yards of the Government road. On the neighbouring estate a coolie was likewise taken while working. Besides this, coolies have been and are regularly taken from Asiatic-owned estates and the surrounding kampongs."

And what an insight into the colonial civil servant's life in the old days we get in this *Straits Times* leader:

> "Why is the Malayan service so unpopular? Bad pay in the earlier days, long distance from Home, a climate with an evil reputation, and, above all, scandalous abuse of the country by the Imperial authorities ..... until a few years ago a civil servant's life was a constant fight against poverty. It was next to madness to marry before the first grey hairs appeared, and retirement took place without honour on a paltry pension."

The reference there is to the separate civil services of the Straits

Settlements and the F.M.S. These were amalgamated into the Malayan Civil Service after the Great War — the first of the services at the European level to be so reorganised — but evidently it still had a bad name at Home.

The Beginning Of The End

THE NEWS THAT SINGAPORE was to have a naval base came during my first month on the *Straits Times*, and, odd as it may seem, those impressions of the new junior reporter in the Cecil Street office come back now, in a new era of world history, as significant echoes of the time.

May 1, 1923 ..... in our perspective the historic date on which the Navy Estimates introduced in the House of Commons included £11 million for the construction of a naval base in the Straits of Johore. That was the first time that Parliament and the British public were told that the Conservative Government of the day had finally decided to go ahead with the Singapore naval base scheme, which had been mooted since the war, but only as a proposal by the Admiralty.

But it certainly was not seen as an historic date in Singapore. In the *Straits Times* office the only reaction that I recall was one of amusement at the Reuter cable reporting a Labour M.P., one Captain Hay, as asking why the British Government should be spending money on "an immoral and pestilential cesspool of the Far East".

The *Straits Times* had a leader on the news the next day, and A.W. Still was certainly as well qualified to assess its importance as any journalist in London or elsewhere in the British Empire; but as a newcomer I remember being surprised to find that the leader discussed the base solely from the viewpoint of Imperial defence, and had nothing to say about what it might mean for Singapore itself. However, from the comments one heard around town, I am sure that the *Straits Times* reflected the views of the European commercial community as a whole. Nobody was in the least excited about this news, not even particularly interested.

After all, Hong Kong had had a naval base since the last century, and the Colony and the Navy had apparently lived together there quite harmoniously. Why should there be any difference in Singapore? Well, it unfortunately did not work out at all like that with the Services during the second decade between the wars; but there were not the slightest premonitions of things to come in 1923. No doubt the news that the base was to be sited in the Straits of Johore, on the other side of the island — which had not been expected — must have heightened the feeling that this would be a project apart and outside the life of the port-city as its people had always known it.

Even I, the new boy in the office, figured in that low-key editorial treatment of the story. One afternoon during that month of May I was handed the Straits Settlements Government Gazette, which came out on Fridays, and told to look through it to see whether there was anything in those official pages that might make a news item. Well, I did find one: a notice that the Colony Government was going to acquire 1699 acres in the district of Sembawang for the Admiralty. (Later acquisitions brought the total up to 3000 acres).

That got one paragraph on the page allocated to court reports and local sport under the heading "Admiralty and Singapore". That was all the *Straits Times* sub-editors thought the story was worth; but now, two world wars later, we know that that one portentous paragraph was not only the beginning of the naval base but the beginning of the end for colonial Singapore, as recorded in the histories of the World War (though the Japanese would have overrun the Malay Peninsula and taken Singapore whether the base had been built or not, since their main objective

THE BEGINNING OF THE END 213

was the vital oilfields of the Dutch East Indies.)

To those office memories I can now add the thoughts that must have been in my editor's mind as he began to write that leader, for he has documented them himself. In his contribution to the Centenary volumes headed "Singapore's Future" Still quoted an astonishing prophecy by Sir Frank Swettenham before he left Singapore on retirement in 1903. Swettenham, whose long Anglo-Malayan career ended as Governor of the Straits Settlements, said at a banquet given in his honour:

> "You have in Singapore a city of 200,000 inhabitants, which will one day be a million, and a port reckoned by the tonnage of its shipping as the seventh largest in the world. Then you have a magnificent natural harbour on which nothing has yet been spent, but which, if protected by works, would afford 1300 acres of sheltered anchorage. You have wharves and docks which have already won fame beyond these shores, and are capable of great improvement. You have the making of a great naval base which we believe is already almost impregnable....."

Still (who was writing in 1921) followed up that prophecy with the questions — and perhaps the answers — that it raised for him as Singapore entered the second century of its local history:

> "Is Singapore destined to become a great naval base? Tell me how the League of Nations will flourish; how China will break the fetters of Manchuism; how Japan will profit by great lessons from the West; and I will answer that question. Suffice it to say that almost instantly on the outbreak of the Great War in 1914, the headquarters of the China Naval Station were moved to Singapore, and that, outside the British Isles, no

naval command was more vitally important than that which had its shore quarters at Fort Canning."

In 1921 the Prince of Wales (later the tragic King Edward VIII), had visited the Dominions of Australia and New Zealand in the battle cruiser *Renown*; and in 1922 he had come to the Straits and the F.M.S., fresh from the magnificent pageantry of his tour of British India and the Native States. In Singapore, as in Australia and New Zealand, the Prince, then at the height of his popularity — must have seemed a symbol of a mighty Empire, and of a Royal Navy fully capable of protecting it.

Before going on to Hong Kong the Prince of Wales had opened the Malaya-Borneo Exhibition in Singapore, the first of its kind, and that made a great impression too. All the British colonial and imperial power of the region was focussed on Singapore that day.

At the same time, Japan was still thought of in Singapore as the friendly and trustworthy ally of the war years; and the *Straits Times* — unlike the London newspapers I had read in Colchester when it became known that the Committee of Imperial Defence were pressing for a new British base capable of serving a modern battle fleet in the Far East — did not see the Singapore base as intended to be a defensive bastion of the British Empire against Japan. But as an observer of Far Eastern affairs for a quarter of a century none knew better than A.W. Still that Japan was a formidable naval power, and that it could be a potential threat as far south as Singapore in the unforeseeable future.

Still had come to the *Straits Times* from India only six years after the Japanese Navy had annihilated the fleet that the Tsar of Russia had sent halfway round the world in an attempt to rendezvous with his naval forces at Vladivostock. One of Ager's memories was of watching the Great White Fleet steam through the Singapore Strait, after the long voyage around Africa and through the Indian Ocean and on to its doom in the battle of Tshuima Bay. That was the first time that an Asiatic power had challenged a Western one, and the first body blow at European prestige in the Far East, the end of the myth of Western invincibility.

Nevertheless, the British Navy was already calling home its battleships from the China Sea (there had been as many as six at the turn of the century) to meet the growing challenge from the Kaiser's Germany, but also because battleships became too big for the Hong Kong dockyard after the first Dreadnought was launched in 1906 and made all existing capital ships obsolete. Nothing bigger than a cruiser could now be serviced at Hong Kong.

It was the Anglo-Japanese Alliance that made this British withdrawal possible; and during the Great War, when the naval command at Fort Canning was very much aware that there was a Japanese fleet of twelve battleships, eight battlecruisers and twenty-one cruisers in the China Sea, the alliance held firm.

After the war, however, when the new United States Pacific Fleet emerged from the Panama Canal in 1919, and Britain had to give up the Anglo-Japanese Alliance (under pressure from Canada and the United States), it became clear that the balance of naval power in the Pacific had changed, and the nakedness of Britain was only too evident in it.

Japan conceded naval superiority to Britain and the United States in the famous 5 - 5 - 3 ratio for battleships fixed by the Washington Naval Treaty of 1921; and that — together with agreement on where new bases could or could not be built in the Far East — augured well for peace in the Pacific. But the treaty was soon repudiated by new political forces in the United States as well as Japan.

Meanwhile Australia and New Zealand had demanded assurances at the Imperial Conference held in London in 1921 that the Royal Navy could still protect them with a battle fleet in the Pacific in the event of another war.

And so that postwar Conservative Government at Westminster decided that the Singapore base had to be built, as a British naval presence in the Far East, but also to satisfy the two Dominions in the South Pacific by assuring them that a battle fleet could be sent to Singapore in an emergency. But where that fleet was to come from if there was war at the same time in the North Sea and the Mediterranean, nobody was asking in 1923 — least of all the *Straits Times* leader that looked back at the prewar and postwar history that we have been recalling.

37
Endpiece

WHEN I STARTED these collections I intended to look back through the whole period between the wars. But I found myself mining so rich a lode of memory during my first year or two that I felt I had to stay with it, since it is my earliest memories that are, I think, the most curious and the most worth recording of all. So it is the early 1920s that have become the theme and the period of this book.

However, if the reader has been interested in what he has read about Singapore as it was after the Great War and after the Centenary, he or she must be wondering what happened after that, and what were the great changes that were just round the corner. So I feel that I should conclude by giving the reader at least a brief look into the years ahead.

Singapore was now entering upon a period of rapid social and technological change, of civic progress and business development, a new and very different chapter in its local history as the port-city of the Raffles tradition and the capital of the Crown Colony. But in other ways life in Singapore, as reflected in these first recollections of mine, went on unchanged for a few more years.

Those were the last years in which Singapore was for the older residents essentially the same place they had known in their youth, as it had been for their seniors at the turn of the century

..... the last trouble-free, tranquil, busy if quiet years in Raffles Place and Tanglin before the world Depression of the early 1930s and the brief and ominously hectic prosperity fuelled by fears of war that followed it.

As a *Straits Times* reporter my best memories are of the modernisation of the city and suburbs that was now undertaken by the Singapore Municipality (by far the most impressive achievement of local government in the whole period of British administration in Malaya), but also by the Colonial Government.

Other memories in my reporter's notebook of those years are of the motor age in full flood, and of the arrival of the air age on the island.

Some people might say that the air age really started in Singapore when the Australian brothers Ross and Keith Smith, with their two mechanics, landed in a wartime Vickers Vimy bomber in 1919, on the flight which won for them the £10,000 prize offered by Lord Northcliffe's *Daily Mail* to the first airmen to fly from England to Australia, with a time-limit of 30 days. They landed on the old racecourse in Kampong Java Road. But there were no more adventurous flights over the Empire air route, as it came to be known, for some years after that.

For me the air age really begins for Singapore with the stationing of a squadron of Royal Air Force flyingboats in the Straits of Johore and the construction of the R.A.F. base on the Seletar shore in the 1920s. Those developments were seen by civilian residents as obviously significant of things to come in overseas and internal air travel.

But the Naval Base scheme at Seletar made no impact upon the city on the other side of the island during the rest of this decade. It remained virtually a non-base, with successive Labour and Conservative governments at Westminster taking a leisurely and blissfully unconcerned stop-go line for reasons of pacifist ideology or national finance. For civilian Singapore the Naval Base did not become a visible reality until the huge floating dock arrived in the Straits of Johore in 1929, having been towed by Dutch tugs round the Cape from the Tyne shipyard where it was built.

The opening of the Causeway for road traffic in late 1924 — a ceremony performed jointly by the Governor of the Colony and the Sultan of Johore — opened a new chapter in the social history of Singapore. Most travel upcountry on business continued to be by F.M.S. Railways, but even a business trip could now be a new experience if there was time to go by road. For the motoring public in general — a rapidly expanding one in all the racial communities (except the Malays) — life in Singapore now offered more varied and pleasurable possibilities than ever before.

For workers in commercial offices and shops, European and Asiatic, there still was no annual local leave, but it now became possible to explore the Johore hinterland by car on a Sunday, or drive as far as Malacca and back by Negri Sembilan at Chinese New Year or some other holiday weekend. However, I must add that for the four European old-timers in the *Straits Times* office the Johore Causeway seemed to make no difference whatever. They might have driven their wives over to Johore Bahru for a Sunday afternoon *"makan angin"*, but I am sure none of them ever took these new opportunities to see life and scenery in upcountry Malaya. Life for them went on in the same old routine in city and suburbs week after week between one Home leave and another.

One of my first memories of life in Singapore after the Causeway is of the day when several of us drove across the Straits to see the Singapore Municipality's new reservoir on Gunong Kulai, and experienced for the first time the delights of cool jungle heights and mountain scenery within a morning's drive of the city.

If central and northern Malaya were still too distant for many Singapore motorists, European Government officers, who got local leave once a year, could now have an extended tour upcountry — and just think what the local schoolteachers could now do with their holidays, if they could afford a car!

Even the clerical class and the coolie class could now have an outing to Johore Bahru by mosquito-bus. That, I have been told, was a hair-raising experience when the bus drivers had to negotiate the roller-coaster twists and turns of the old Woodlands road. But that was before the European engineers of the Colony P.W.D. not only improved the highway greatly but extended it through the Marsiling swamps to the Straits. However, it was some years before there were regular bus services from Singapore on the trunk road through the Peninsula. The direct route north from Ayer Hitam did not then exist, so all road travel north necessarily included the Batu Pahat and Muar river ferries.

The widening and lengthening of Singapore's Malayan horizons was only a gradual process; and the historical framework in which the city people thought of public affairs and their own way of life was still the Colony, as against the F.M.S. But it was now possible for the car-owning class to go farther and farther afield, and a whole new world of town and country life, of coastal plains and lovely valleys and the majestic mountains of the Main Range, was now opening up for at least the middle and upper classes of Asiatic Singapore, and for the European birds-of-passage of which I was one.

In the *Straits Times* office during this decade there were great changes, and real journalistic progress. After A.W. Still retired in 1926, the influence and status of the *Straits Times* suddenly collapsed like a pricked ballon. Everything had depended on "Still's leader"; and now that editorial column was no better than any other, perhaps not as good. For years the company's board of directors searched overseas for a suitable successor, but it could find no-one able to take Still's place.

I remember a wild character named Major Foran, who had been a big-game hunter in Africa. One evening he got into a fight in the Seaview Hotel bar, and unfortunately the new editor got beaten — surely the lowest point of *Straits Times* prestige between the wars. There was a fine editor who had been the *London Times* staff correspondent in Cairo; and he might have made his mark if he had not died of cancer soon after his appointment. Then the editor of the *Straits Echo* an esteemed Anglo-Malayan editor of the old school, was brought from Penang ..... but Singapore was not Penang. What the *Straits Times* needed after the Great War was modernisation, and that is what none of these importations could give it.

However, in the end the right man was found: G.W. Seabridge, then news editor of the Calcutta Statesman, who had edited a Sunday paper in London, and who brought the technique of Fleet Street to Cecil Street. He set out to bid for mass circulation, mainly by introducing a popular news-magazine content and features in the paper, also greatly improving its racing coverage, and before long he was able to give his readers a much better Reuter cable service as well, thanks to the Empire Press penny-a-word rate from London, subsidised by the British Government.

All this came at the right time, when the English-educated public for newspapers was rapidly growing, thanks to the new English schools of the Colonial Government and expansion in the Roman Catholic, Methodist, Anglican and Presbyterian mission schools as well.

By the time my first agreement with the *Straits Times* was up I had had enough of Singapore and its humid heat, and of European life in the East generally, and was thinking of trying my luck on a newspaper in a temperate climate elsewhere in the British Empire. But I was offered such tempting terms for a second three-year agreement that I could not decline it — and that was the point of no return in any Malayan career.

A Personal Postscript

IN 1927 I WENT ON Home leave for the first time. I went back to England via the Pacific and the United States, and, believe it or not, I travelled the whole way from Hong Kong to Southampton for £75 (about 600 Straits dollars).

Six months leave ended with return via Suez on a one-class N.Y.K. (Japanese) passenger ship, and that has left a mental picture that time has never erased. On the first night out from Southampton, going down the stairs to the dining saloon, I saw on the opposite stairs a pretty girl in evening dress, her eyes bright with anticipation at the prospect of her first voyage to the romantic East, of this adventure that lay ahead of her and that was her honeymoon. But her young husband turned out to be black. As an Indian medical student in Edinburgh, he had married his landlady's daughter, and was taking her back to his family and his home in Singapore.

The colour bar came down instantly in that dining saloon and on the promenade deck. The young bride was completely ostracised by the British women passengers, the husband by the men (myself included). Their only friends during the whole voyage, the only ones ever seen sitting beside them in their deckchairs, were two British prison warders and their wives going back from Home leave to Colombo. My conscience pricked me throughout the voyage (and, judging by one or two muttered remarks I heard on deck, others would have said the same), but as a young man I was afraid of unpopularity with the older passengers, and I never spoke to the young couple. I have never ceased to be ashamed of the moral cowardice of not offering friendship to that homesick Scottish girl and her Indian husband.

When the ship berthed at Tanjong Pagar the Indian family were all there, lined up on the wharf, the womenfolk in their saris. Obviously a conservative, traditional Indian middle-class family. I caught a glimpse of the Scottish bride occasionally after that, in Raffles Place or other public places, and by then she too was wearing the sari and living entirely within the Hindu community.

Those early years in Singapore were my bachelor years, also my years as a junior member of the European community, and that may explain why there is so little in these recollections about social events and the social life of the European community at more affluent levels. But I was very fortunate in being admitted into a circle of lively and friendly young Americans, teachers with U.S. degrees in the Methodist Mission Schools — mostly girls, but several young men as well. Living entirely without alcohol and cigarettes — phenomenal austerity in the Singapore of that day — and with such youthful frivolities as hotel tea-dances also frowned upon by their Methodist superiors, these young Americans insulated in a missionary world of their own thoroughly enjoyed themselves in lighthearted parties and delightful picnics that remain among my pleasantest memories.

One of them was a newly arrived teacher named Lora Buel, and we became engaged. In 1929 I left Singapore to take charge of a new branch office that the *Straits Times* had opened in Kuala Lumpur, and we were married there in Wesley Church on Petaling Hill in 1930. We went on Home leave after that, and came back to Kuala Lumpur. The next three years there were the best of my journalistic life, as the first *Straits Times* staff man to be stationed in the old Federal capital indeed the only Straits Settlements journalist from any paper working outside the Colony. As the job developed, it proved to be a roving commission in the F.M.S., with excursions into Trengganu and Kelantan as well. It was altogether a marvellously educative experience for an Anglo-Malayan journalist at that stage in my career.

In 1934 my wife and I returned to Singapore, with a baby son born in the old European Hospital in Kuala Lumpur. This was an institution in which all the nursing was done by European sisters, and which had become so indefensible in its colonial discrimination against the other racial communities, that it was abolished soon afterwards. A daughter and another son were born in Singapore, where we lived in Mount Rosie Road, off Chancery Lane. I discovered who the original Rosie was: a Eurasian girl who married a wealthy German merchant in the 1890s and became his hostess in lavish entertaining of European society in the mansion he built on Mount Rosie, and which in my time was known as Flagstaff House, being the official residence of the British army general always referred to as the G.O.C.

I was now assistant editor of the *Straits Times*. My reporting days were over, and I was writing leaders, doing sub-editing, and writing a daily column — mostly at home in my spare time, at the sacrifice of my family life — under the nom de plume *Anak Singapura*. Only a journalist who really had been born in Singapore had any right to use the name "Son of Singapore", but at the time it was meant to express my attempt to identify myself with the place, to find something more satisfying than the rootless, transient, superficial way of life, between one Home leave and the next, that one saw in the European commercial and official community. That attempt, so far as I was concerned, only ended up with me sitting on the fence as a Singapore journalist but also as a parent and a citizen, as it must inevitably do for any European or American expatriate who intends to educate and bring up his children in his own native land overseas.

That last decade between the wars was increasingly overshadowed by the Nazi threat in Europe and the imperialist expansion of Japan into China, also locally by the rapid completion of the Singapore Naval Base and the militarisation of the island as more and more regiments and air squadrons poured in from Britain, India and Australia. It was in those years that the old Singapore of Straits Settlements times finally faded away.

On the outbreak of war in Europe on 3 September 1939, I left the *Straits Times* office in Cecil Street, on loan to the Straits Settlements Government, to take over the new wartime post of Director of Information, Malaya.

In 1940, as the danger of war in the Pacific grew ever more ominous, and on confidential advice available to me in my office in the Cathay Building, I persuaded my reluctant wife to take herself and our three young children to the safety of her parents' home in the United States.

In early 1941 I was given four months leave — what would have been due to me at that time on the *Straits Times* — the fear of Japan entering the war having temporarily receded by then; and I went to Sydney, where my wife joined me from the United States with the children and, thank God, stayed there for the duration of the war.

In Darwin, on the flight back to Singapore, the news came through that the United States had banned the export of oil to Japan, in retaliation for her invasion of French Indochina, and I knew then that war had become almost a certainty.

On December 9, 1941, the Japanese army landed on the coast of Thailand and Kelantan, and on February 15, 1942, Singapore surrendered to General Yamashita. From the Cathay Building I watched the Japanese guns and tanks roll down Selegie Road on their way to the docks for the invasion of Java, and I saw the first Japanese soldier in that building the next day.

I spent three and a half years in the internment camp in Changi Gaol and later in the Sime Road Camp. After the Japanese occupation, Singapore — from the prewar British colonial point of view — was never the same again.

When the British Military Administration took over I stayed on for six weeks, with several other *Straits Times* journalists, who had been in the civilian or POW camps, to get the paper going again. The first issue was given away in the streets amid general rejoicing.

I was flown to Sydney by the R.A.A.F. for recuperation and a blissful reunion with the family and relatives, and went back to Singapore and the *Straits Times* as its first editor after the World War. This time, however, it was not a question of sitting on the fence, as before the war, but of walking the tightrope, as recalled in the preface to this book. Those six years as editor were the last of my career on the *Straits Times* though I have been back several times since.

In this chapter we have come a long way since the early 1920s. The changes one sees in the Singapore of today must make some of what I have written here sound unbelievable and almost fantastic. But my purpose in writing these recollections has been nothing more ambitious than to offer some relaxation to the people who have to endure the pace and noise and strain of city life today. To leave behind a personal record for posterity's sake of the distant, now almost legendary past.